Domagoj Kostanjšak

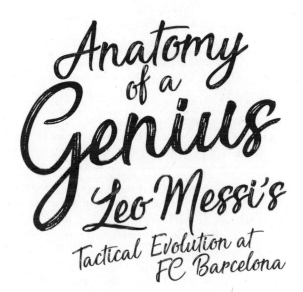

Anatomy
of a
Genius
Leo Messi's
Tactical Evolution at
FC Barcelona

pitch

First published by Pitch Publishing, 2022

Pitch Publishing
9 Donnington Park,
85 Birdham Road,
Chichester,
West Sussex,
PO20 7AJ
www.pitchpublishing.co.uk
info@pitchpublishing.co.uk

ISBN 978 1 80150 181 1

Typesetting and origination by Pitch Publishing
Printed and bound in India by Replika Press Pvt. Ltd.

Contents

To my loving family for their unfaltering support and to Željka, my muse and my rock. Without you, this book would have been impossible.

And to FC Barcelona and Lionel Messi, the source of many sleepless nights and moments of joy.

Thank you.

Foreword

DO YOU really need to read another book about Lionel Messi?
Well, yes: this one.

Messi's story isn't exactly a secret. You probably already know the details of his boyhood in Rosario, followed by his emotional teenage move to Barcelona. Then his early breakthrough into senior football with a large debt of thanks to the selfless guidance of Ronaldinho, followed by a full flowering into superstardom under the inspired management of Pep Guardiola.

After that came Messi's hugely successful reinvention alongside Luis Suárez and Neymar, before he attempted to almost single-handedly stave off Barça's long and sad decline until his departure to Paris Saint-Germain that left fans – and, it appears, Messi himself – stunned and speechless.

Simultaneously, the tale of Messi's international career with Argentina has been one of ups and downs. Great early successes in the 2005 World Youth Championship and the 2008 Olympics were followed by more than a decade of frustrating and often bitter disappointments, before his long-awaited first senior international trophy finally arrived with the 2021 Copa América.

Away from his achievements on the pitch, the details of Messi's personal life are also well known – his marriage to childhood sweetheart Antonella and fatherhood of three boys, which played a big part in eventually allowing him to leave behind his shy and introverted teenage self and mature into a confident and composed adult.

So if you already know these details of Messi's story, as most football fans do, why should you bother to read this book? Very simply, because it's different from any I've seen before.

In the pages that follow, Domagoj Kostanjšak guides us through the story of Messi's career with the specific approach of explaining how he did it. And therein lies the difference: whereas other studies on the Argentine genius generally tend to describe his greatness, this book analyses it.

In particular, I find it fascinating to delve more deeply into how Messi has evolved his playing style over the years – from an inverted winger under Frank Rijkaard to a false 9 under Pep Guardiola, before reverting to a different kind of winger in the 'MSN' (Messi, Suárez, Neymar) forward line and finally ending up as a deeper-lying playmaker as the team around him imploded. Domagoj does a terrific job in both chronicling those various stages of Messi's career and, with the help of easily understood and well-explained tactical diagrams, analysing precisely how he functioned within the wider context of Barça's overall team structures at the time.

Reading this book will bring back many memories of Messi's genius. It certainly did for me. I've been blessed by the fortune of living in Barcelona since 2012, visiting the Camp Nou on a regular basis. In the first game I ever attended in a working capacity, Messi scored twice in the opening 16 minutes as his team thrashed Real Sociedad 5-1. That was a suitably brilliant prelude for countless afternoons and evenings spent perched high in the press box at Barça's gradually crumbling but still awe-inspiring home, revelling in the unmatched majesty of Messi at his long-lasting peak.

Messi's capacity to produce a sudden piece of magic that takes your breath away – no matter how many times you've seen him do similar things – is unmatched by the thousands of other athletes I've ever seen. Many thrilling memories immediately come to my mind, and none more so than an electrifying evening in May 2015, when he dismantled the mighty Bayern Munich – coached by his former mentor Guardiola – with two brilliant goals in the space of four minutes, including a dazzling dribble to leave Jerome Boateng flat on his backside before floating a glorious right-footed chip over a stunned Manuel Neuer.

When he scored that second goal, and on many more occasions, all I could do was shake my head and wonder how on earth he did it. And in this book, Domagoj gives us some of the answers (not all of them, of course – genius can never be fully accounted for, or it wouldn't be genius).

How did he play alongside Ronaldinho in those early days? How exactly did Guardiola's revolutionary false 9 system actually work? Why, other than their undeniable individual brilliance, were the 'MSN' trio able to enjoy so much success? How did Messi attempt to – often successfully – paper over the cracks of his team's decline during the last few years of his Camp Nou career? If you want to know the answers to those questions and many more, read on.

Football analysis can be a divisive topic. Many traditionalists lament the introduction of occasionally oblique terms such as expected goals per 90, medium blocks and counter-pressing, arguing that football is a simple, free-flowing game and that analytics too often descends into unnecessarily complicated and pretentious jargon. Many other fans, conversely, find immense value in the exercise of trying to explain how the intricate movements of 22 players and one ball all fit together, providing a greater understanding of why goals actually happen.

With Domagoj, we have the best of both worlds. He has the rare and valuable ability to analyse players and teams without getting himself (and his readers) lost in a forest of information, picking out the key points and keeping his insights clear, concise and easy to understand. He's one of the best football analysts you'll find, and in this book he's tackling the greatest player of our times. A perfect combination, which I'm sure will leave you enthralled, entertained and informed.

Andy West

Preface

I'VE ALWAYS wanted to write a book, and yet never thought I would actually do it. As much as writing has always been a passion of mine, ever since my early childhood, the actual process seemed much too daunting to ever attempt. After all, *'What would I even write about?'* I thought to myself. And to be completely honest, it wasn't until about a year and a half ago that I found the answer to that question. The dawn of 2022 marks the start of my fourth year in sports writing, or tactical analysis to be more precise. And this is where my true story begins as well. Up until somewhere in 2018, I was just a casual football fan, watching matches and stressing over a team I had picked to support approximately 20 years ago. But back when I first started, I had no idea why my team was successful or rubbish at times, nor did I pay much attention to it either.

In came *Total Football Analysis* and Chris Darwen in the summer of 2018. Little did I know that joining their LaLiga and Barcelona teams would impact the direction of my upcoming career. It was around that time that I started focusing on the small print of football matches, analysing what made teams tick as well as what made them fall apart. Back then, analysis, scouting and data were all largely unknown terms for me, but over the years I've honed my trade, and can proudly say that since the moment Chris first answered my email in 2018, I've grown a lot and been blessed with jobs at different companies and even professional clubs.

But while *Total Football Analysis* was definitely my first attempt at tactical analysis, my first encounter with professional sports writing or reporting came some years before that, back in Croatia. For a while I spent my days writing news and opinion articles for a site called SportArena, led by my project manager and first boss, Ivan Žeželj. It was he who first introduced me to this vast world of football and moulded me both as a writer and as a person behind the huge chunks of text. I'll never forget him yelling at me (kindly, of course): 'Real sports journalists have a Twitter account, go open one!' So I did. Through Twitter and a growing audience, my reach and influence rose and, as much as you can call it that, so did my success. His early guidance is something I cherish to this day. All of that, of course, culminated with this book on none other than Lionel Messi.

But why Messi and why Barcelona? Interestingly, it's the case of a very familiar trope with young boys where their fathers influence a great portion of their hobbies and early interests. Around 20 years ago, my father walked into the room with two different jerseys he had previously bought from god knows where. They had no names on the back but were also completely different: one was a Chelsea shirt, slick, shiny and all draped in blue, while the other was a *Blaugrana* FC Barcelona shirt with clear blue-and-garnet features that would ultimately change my life.

It was on that day that my father decided I would be a Barcelona fan while my younger brother Juraj would become a Chelsea fan. The rest, as they say, is history. I always look back at that moment and giggle at the fact I could have easily been writing a book on the London Blues now, had my father made a slightly different decision on that fateful day. But I'm glad he didn't, for better or worse.

From then on started a 20-year-long journey, with ups and downs, countless late nights watching Champions League football with very limited LaLiga coverage back in Croatia but also with so much joy along the way. For a while, interestingly, I was so much into Barcelona that my father decided to make me a member, securing it somehow when I was a kid and then framing it on the wall once the letter had finally arrived. But since we were living in Croatia back then, far from the glamour of the Camp Nou, there wasn't much I got from that rather expensive experience other than an annual Barça poster for my birthday and, of course, ultimate bragging rights in school. Sadly, it didn't last, and soon after we had to cancel it, never renewing again.

It's actually quite interesting that my family, especially my father, has been so supportive of my love for the Catalan club. After all, apart from my grandpa Ivo on my mother's side, there's not a single other *Culé* in the family. My brother is a Chelsea Blue, while neither my cousins nor my mother have much interest in football nowadays, and my father, believe it or not, loves Manchester United; what a merry combination of clubs in our household. So a huge hug to my grandpa Ivo, who will no doubt do his best to read this book.

Still, as I've said, my father has been eternally supportive of my love for Barcelona, so naturally I've had my fair share of football kits back home as well. The first name I had on the back of a shirt was, of course, Ronaldinho, but soon the likes of Xavi, Puyol and Messi would follow. Leo was still a youngster breaking through when I first started following Barça but I grew up alongside him. And regardless of whether he was my favourite player donning the *Blaugrana* colours or not (which, surprisingly, he isn't), his emergence and evolution played a big part in my love for the club over the years. So my focus had to be Barcelona first, and then, following that same line of thought, it simply had to be Messi too. The greatest to ever play football for my greatest achievement (so far) as an author.

But if something has always bugged me about the narrative surrounding Leo, it's the perception of a great player never leaving his comfort zone or proving himself in different systems and structures. As a tactical mind, this was something I wanted to personally rectify. So I did, expressing it through what I loved the most: writing. That's how this book came to be, through a union of my two passions of Barça and writing, with a subtle blend of tactical nuance and personal stakes on the line.

Many have made this possible, not least the people to first provide me with a platform to create. Both Chris Darwen and Ivan Žeželj are my original mentors, the latter being one of my number one fans as well. For that, I'm eternally grateful. Friends and family have been very supportive, although I've kept this book a secret from almost all of them, wanting it to be a surprise.

I want to thank the following people for their invaluable chats and long answers to complicated questions, as well as enduring some of my ramblings and opinions: Álex Delmás, Albert Blaya, Michael Cox, Samuel Marsden, Jordi Costa, Sid Lowe and Graham Hunter. Your insight has made this book possible in the first place. Along the same lines, I have to mention Taher Mortezaie, someone who's actually worked for the club for years and has been kind enough to share some of that experience with me. I've deeply enjoyed our conversation about La Masia and I've come out a far more knowledgeable analyst with a much better understanding of the club and its processes.

A special mention goes to one of the most talented authors and someone I consider a friend at this stage, Andy West. Andy has provided me with contacts, quotes and a brilliantly heartwarming foreword for the book. I can only hope my writing warrants such praise and the effort he's put into it. People such as Abhishek Sharma (@abhisheksh_98) and Maram AlBaharna (@maramperninety) were in charge of making the book's visuals come to life and have done an amazing job of it – a huge thank you to them for that. The same goes for an incredibly talented artist and graphic designer Aljohara, 'Al', also known as Barça Pictures #14 (@Barca__pictures), who made some stunning covers for the book's promotional purposes.

Similarly, I have to say thanks to Andrew Flint, my editor and great friend, who did his best to make sense of my thoughts and actually succeeded in turning them into a cohesive unit, an effort not to be easily dismissed. *Spasibo*, my Russian friend! Intriguingly, for a while during my college years, I was losing my interest in Barcelona and a very kind and knowledgeable individual named Silvija Kraljić, a long-term fan herself, helped me spark it once more. Without us sharing this seemingly meaningless interest, who knows whether I would have even remained a passionate fan to this day. Thank you, S, I truly appreciate that.

Finally, I want to mention three other individuals whose chats and support can hardly be put into words. Abdullah, Toni Bilandžić – who also made some amazing-looking graphs for me – and Scott Martin have become some of my best friends and I never would have even met them had I not gone on this journey of tactical analysis and sports writing. Thank you for your thoughts, conversations, insight and immediate feedback. One couldn't wish for better friends. On the other spectre of things, there's my loving mother, who, to be completely honest, knows very little about football. But due to Leo often being in TV commercials and me yapping on about him whenever an opportunity arose, she just asks whether 'Señor Messi' is playing whenever she sees me watch a match. So yes, Mum, this is indeed a book on 'Señor Messi' – I hope you'll like it. My father, on the other hand, has more football knowledge than I'll ever hope to have or would even dream to argue, and he's proven instrumental on this journey of mine – for turning me into a *Culé*, supporting my fanboy years while I couldn't do it myself, and for making me fall in love with the game, even if it's just through the written word. Thank you, Dad – I hope this makes you proud.

And then there's the love of my life and my rock through stormy weather. Željka Gosarić is the ideal partner in crime but she's also so much more than that. Saying I wouldn't have been able to do this without her would probably be the biggest understatement you'll find in these pages. When she was younger, she kept saying how her only wish was that her future husband didn't like football. Whoops. But I'm proud to say that she's coping with it bravely and can even name some Barcelona players now, past and present! I love you, Ž, and I can't wait for you to read this book.

Of course, I have to mention Barcelona and Messi himself as the ultimate inspirations behind the first, and hopefully not last, book of my career. Without their influence, it's safe to say you wouldn't be holding this in your hands. For that, I thank them. All of these people have played a role in making this little dream possible – in that sense, this book is as much theirs as it is mine. Through it, I wanted to show both my passion and, hopefully, my knowledge. It's a unique take on a very familiar topic and is aimed at casual fans and *tácticos* alike. Last but not least, a shout out to Pitch Publishing for agreeing to help me turn this into reality – thank you, good people.

Hopefully you'll enjoy reading *Anatomy of a Genius: Leo Messi's Tactical Evolution at FC Barcelona* as much as I did writing it. Here's to many more and as ever – *Força Barça*!

Introduction

The Many Faces of Leo

PROBABLY THE biggest misconception about Lionel Messi's career is the narrative of the Argentine hiding in his comfort zone at Barcelona his whole life. His greatest critics will always point that out as the major shortcoming of an otherwise stellar career, claiming he's only ever had to play within the same system throughout his stay at the Camp Nou. However, even if we disregard the fact that Messi had to face the greatest challenge of leaving his home and family behind at an early age, injecting himself with growth hormones as a child and crying himself to sleep every night, that statement would still be incredibly far from the truth. Over the years, we've seen him grow from a timid and yet brilliant talent to a spark in Barcelona's modern revolution and then, finally, to their and the world's greatest player. And somewhere along the way, he and Barcelona both had to change.

Change isn't always easy but it's also often necessary for survival. From the moment he stepped on to the pitch for Frank Rijkaard's Barcelona, Messi had to adapt his game. In his youth, he was a left-winger or even an *enganche*, the traditional No.10, but since his favourite positions were occupied by stars much bigger than him at that time, he was relegated to the right. Playing on the side opposite to that of your dominant foot is incredibly difficult and requires a complete change of approach. From movement, dribbling, shooting or even just positioning in relation to the ball and other players around him, everything was different. Next came the transition to the now-famous false 9 role under Pep Guardiola. By that time, Messi had already become one of the best players in the world despite still being just a youngster. With that in mind, a complete overhaul of his player profile wasn't necessary as it's reasonable to assume he would have had a fairly decent career as a winger too.

But Pep thought the next stage of his evolution required another tweak and Messi was courageous enough to not only accept it but also to try it out against Barcelona's eternal rivals, Real Madrid. That's the very definition of leaving your comfort zone and experimenting. Needless to say, it was a risk that ultimately paid off and paved the way for the best version of the Argentine magician we would ever see. But it wasn't the most complete one just yet. Sure, his goalscoring ability skyrocketed and so did his importance, influence and reputation. But that doesn't cover the fact that it was mostly uncharted territory for Leo at that level, even though playing centrally and between the lines with freedom wasn't entirely new to him.

As Michael Cox, author and analyst, mentions, it was actually Tito Vilanova who experimented with such set-ups while Messi was still in the youth teams. Cox told me when we discussed the Argentine's most important coaches:

> I think it's worth pointing out that Tito Vilanova had him as a youngster and was very good with him at that point. I think I'm right in saying that Vilanova had fielded him as a central forward in one of the youth teams and, therefore, as assistant to Guardiola was

probably important in suggesting he could be used there for the first team.

With bags of talent at his disposal, Messi was always very good at adapting to different scenarios and challenges.

After Guardiola's departure from the club, the next big evolution came during Luis Enrique Martínez García's stint at the Camp Nou. This period gave us the first glimpse of the total player Messi was gearing up to become, one that not only scores bags of goals but is ready to take up the mantle of a creator, sometimes even willingly taking a back seat so others, particularly Neymar Jr. and Luis Suárez, could shine a bit more. This saw Messi shift from the false 9 back to the inverted winger role to accommodate El Pistolero's (Suárez's) arrival. Even though it meant he would be moving away from a position that had made him the superstar he already was, he recognised that change was for the benefit of everyone, somewhat reluctantly surrendering the central role to Suárez.

The final stage of Messi's Barcelona evolution includes him becoming the absolute centre of the team in every imaginable way. Sadly, as his importance rose, that of others declined until he was the only spark in an otherwise bleak and uninspired team. But as important and as recurring as position changes would become for Messi over the years, that wasn't the only challenge that was posed to him.

The ultimate challenge was to constantly adapt to the demands and needs of the game and the players surrounding him. That's what the biggest talents do; they recognise what the team lacks and find solutions to that specific issue. Whether that's done by altering their own style or through other means is ultimately up to them. 'More than adapting to different structures, I guess he adapted to the qualities of his team-mates,' Jordi Costa explained when we discussed this aspect of Leo's profile. Every single stage of his career brought about a change that was sparked by a necessity of some sort. Whether it was the team needing a brand-new approach to make use of the opposition's flaws or whether they needed an elite creator in the absence of such profiles in the squad, Messi was there to help.

Sid Lowe, author, journalist and LaLiga expert, told me:

> First, you get Messi the guy that runs at people. Then you've got Messi the guy that scores goals. Then you get Messi the guy that runs across the front of people, from right to left. Then you get Messi the guy that delivers that pass to Jordi Alba on the left-hand side. This is the guy that's the best dribbler, the best finisher, the best passer in the game in all of those things. You can see different stages of Messi's career and evolutionary process, which speaks very highly of his level of completeness.

Indeed, you can see very clearly that Messi had absolutely had to change his personal approach to accommodate for the team's issues. But it's not only him that's changed over the years.

We also have to tackle the sheer disparity between all the coaches Messi outlasted at the club. From Rijkaard to Ronald Koeman, every single one of them had their own idea of how to manage both Messi and the rest of the team. Some of them did it with more success than others. But regardless of their approach, whether it was all-out guns blazing attacking football or pragmatic opportunism, Leo adapted to it all. Not only that, but he excelled in every single one of those structures. 'He's absolutely had to play under different systems and had to adapt to different circumstances in his career. If you look at how Barcelona played under Pep Guardiola and how they played under Ernesto Valverde, they're completely different teams,' explains, journalist and LaLiga expert Samuel Marsden.

This not only tells us that Messi had to change his approach countless times for the better of the team, but that he also had to alter his own approach to excel in whatever new aspects coaches had brought to the table at that time. The only comfort zone we can talk about is the psychological one of being in the same city and the same setting for the majority of his life. His early struggles at Paris Saint-Germain (PSG) are largely tactical but the personal trauma of such an involuntary and abrupt change has definitely played a part too. All of this and more is true for his career with the national team as well, but that's a different topic altogether.

Now, however, it's time to sink our teeth into the incredible evolution of Messi's profile at Barcelona over the years, starting with his early academy and La Masia days.

Let's get straight into it.

Chapter 1

La Masia's Finest

IT'S NO secret that Lionel Messi's first steps at Barcelona were rather difficult. Of course, signing for a club thousands of miles away from his home and having to leave his family behind was always going to impact the adaptation period. Despite his glaringly obvious talent, there's no denying that the club was taking a big risk by investing so much in a boy that was an unknown quantity back then. His medical condition aside, Messi was a frail and timid child arriving at a club that had global aspirations.

Times were still far from ideal in Catalonia and it would take them some years to get back to the top with Frank Rijkaard and Ronaldinho leading the modern revolution of the *Azulgranas*. Messi, of course, would be a huge part of that rallying charge too, but not many would have predicted that when he first joined the academy. I asked Graham Hunter, journalist, author, analyst and LaLiga expert, whether there was an indication of greatness about Leo in the early stages of his Barcelona career. He explained:

> Greatness is too strong of a word because what it
> definitely was right from the first instant was a real

clarity that he was extraordinary. When he first arrived [at Barcelona], he was timid and silent to the extent that people worried about his personality. And remember, he was tiny. While Messi always did things that showed he had more skill, more technique than any of the other players and always did things that stunned people, the entire collection of things that would make him truly great didn't really become very clear until 2004 or 2005.

His road from being a talented individual to La Masia's finest was rocky and long. Of course, as time went on, it became increasingly more difficult to ignore his potential. As Hunter points out, he always had more skill and more technique than anyone else. Sometimes, however, that isn't enough.

La Masia's success became evident during Pep Guardiola's tenure at the club but their principles were well defined by that point already. When scouting for players, Barcelona look at several key aspects that a young player must show, including how good their technique is and how well they understand and see the game. There are more, of course, but generally speaking, these two are traits you'll find in almost every academy graduate at the club. But this also doesn't mean it's all they're good at. Every player is unique so inevitably some will come with a lot of speed, strength or with an incredible eye for a pass or goal. Those traits are immediately identified and then groomed.

However, young players are never finished products and every single one comes with strengths and weaknesses together. This is very important to understand because no one could have predicted Messi's unbelievable development into a total player. Granted, a lot of it was innate talent and love for the game but a lot also comes from proper development and coaching in the early years of his career. 'The way that we like to develop them [young players at La Masia] is helping them to grow the bottom level,' said Albert Capellas, ex-coordinator of Barcelona's Academy, in an interview for *Inside the Academy*. The bottom level here means traits they're not necessarily that good at. Often, physical traits aside, La Masia graduates are very well-rounded players; they're players of great technique, vision, reading and understanding of the game and positional play. This is no coincidence either as the club works hard to create such profiles in the first place. Barcelona scouts recognise great talent and extraordinary skill in players but then coaches at the club refine their basic skills, skills that ultimately help them play simply. 'Doing exceptional things is talent – that's scouting. But helping them to play simple – that's coaching,' explained Capellas in the same interview.

Barcelona never taught Messi to be extraordinary in that sense. But they did help him harness the innate talent and transform it into something more palpable and suitable to both his personal player profile and also to serve the collective at a higher level. La Masia does very well to improve on players' flaws, or just tries to mould them into positions and roles that cater to their strengths. Everything starts from there. Instead of looking for players who immediately fit the philosophy, it's about identifying young and talented players and then coaching them to maximise that.

We can apply the same process to Messi himself. When Barcelona first scouted him, he was this scrawny kid who could dribble past the entire opposition team without batting an eyelid and then score. Clearly, the extraordinary talent was already visible. But he was very raw, running at players with his head down and beating them through sheer skill and difference in individual quality. 'Gradually he got taught the ways of Barcelona in terms of completely understanding the positional play, the triangles, pressing and moving,' Hunter explained. Coaching for young Messi wasn't necessarily extremely important. He didn't watch a lot of football in the early years of his career and didn't really care for analysis. His talent was so big that for the majority of his youth days it was enough to make the difference. 'While he was younger, people were trying to coach him and change him and he just ignored them,' continued Hunter.

But *that* Messi is miles behind the one we would eventually enjoy watching on the big screen or at the grandest of stages. The difference, once again, is in doing the simple things well. Of course, nothing Messi does is ever that simple. But his basics are on an extremely high level: controlling the ball, passing, vision and even shooting. All of those things are traits every footballer should work on, regardless of their position or style of play of the team. And they're also traits that are developed at La Masia. I was lucky enough to speak to Taher Mortezaie, the current technical and project director at Barça Academy Brisbane, who's been working for the club for years, even spending three years as a coach in their academy. While he's never trained Messi directly, he helped me understand some key elements of coaching within Barcelona's academy and La Masia as well.

That's actually the first big point we need to understand. Barcelona's academy and La Masia are not the same thing. People often get it wrong and confuse one with the other. However, while both can include players of similar age, the main difference is in the level of competitiveness. Mortezaie explained during our chat:

> The main difference is that La Masia is 100 per cent competitive from six or seven years old onward. Of course, the academy is competitive as well, but this

period is more about education and trials because it's very difficult to get in [La Masia]. So the two will regularly swap players between six and 12 years old.

In a way, the academy is La Masia for La Masia. Therefore, in an ideal world, a player's usual path of development will then be the academy – La Masia – first team.

Interestingly, so much of what Mortezaie has told me echoes Capellas's words too. La Masia tries to mould players in a certain way, prioritising some key traits of their player profiles. But at the same time, as Mortezaie explains, two other aspects are absolutely fundamental in their approach – freedom and personal development:

> In the beginning, we taught children different aspects of the game in different blocks, each very deep and detailed for a thing X, Y or Z. But this is not always so. Barcelona are not very linear in their approach to training because how can you specifically prepare for scenarios A, B or C when football, just like life, is such chaos most of the time? So we would still go through blocks of training but give players more freedom of how and when we want to implement it into the training sessions.

It's more about the freedom of choice here. Players are put in different scenarios that are likely to occur on the pitch and then observed as they take action in certain ways to find the best possible solution to a given problem. That's what develops their understanding of the game while also building up their agency. It's not so much about telling them what's the right or wrong way to play, but rather helping them understand what benefits them and the collective in specific scenarios, according to Mortezaie:

Instead of telling them what way is best, we tell them to assess what options they have in any given scenario. And that's what we do — we create options for them for every situation and foster awareness — not, you did something wrong, but rather, understanding why you did something and have you thought about whether it helps you and your team-mates.

Of course, while he can't tell me that was exactly what Barcelona did with Messi, it's fair to assume it did play a part in fostering Leo's development towards a more complete profile that not only highlights his incredible talent, but also aims to maximise it for the benefit of the collective.

The freedom of expression helps coaches understand what the player is like and what their main traits are. With Messi, it was quite clear he was a dribbler of exceptional technical quality. But it came with a lot of caveats too, one of which is being very individualistic in his approach. Mortezaie actually indirectly talks about handling that very aspect in young players:

To outsiders, it might seem very rigid — pass the ball, one-touch football and such — but it's more about creating sessions where children can express themselves. Rather than tell them 'pass, dribble or do that', you create an environment where different players can express themselves in different ways. So if a player takes a lot of risk during sessions, instead of calling him out for doing that, we try to see why he does it and what benefits or attitudes it can give the team. Also, is it something we have to work on or is it a trait that can develop in the future so you'd want him to feel that freedom and take the risk?

There's absolutely no doubt that Barcelona recognised Leo's strengths very early on, and then it was all about building on them, for both parties' sake. But academy graduates are people first, and children at that, players second, so how you approach their development matters a lot. La Masia builds the player by building the person behind that player first. We all know how Messi, in particular, is an introvert, which was even more obvious when he was a kid. External circumstances such as leaving home at an early age and being far away from his family definitely played a part in moulding his personality too, but there's no escaping the fact that he was genuinely a silent and shy boy.

At the beginning, he didn't even live in La Masia along with the other children but instead in a nearby flat with his father. When he was around other people from the club, he was a mostly quiet and unassuming soul. However, in time, he came out of his shell to eventually become one of the popular ones. Hunter recalls:

> As he slowly got accustomed to life in Barcelona, he became a really well-liked kid. People in school would do some of his homework for him or would just give him answers for stuff. He was definitely popular for his character more than just because he was a great footballer at that age. He was very brave.

This is also something La Masia puts a lot of emphasis on – developing the character, the person behind the scenes.

Needless to say, Messi needed a lot of that upon first arriving at the club. The key is to help the children feel safe and comfortable. So many of them come with all sorts of different baggage or issues they're trying to repress, sweep under the rug or somehow overcome. The sooner the club realises that and tends to the person first rather than the player, the better for all of them.

Developing Messi's character and personality, especially in the early stages of his career, was as important as harnessing his godly potential. Mortezaie explains:

> Football can be played in many different ways, but it's not just about the football that's played at a club, it's about seeing players as human beings with different personalities and needs. Once you understand that person, their dreams and fears, then you have a big chance to both influence the player and the person.

This is the fundamental thing across all levels of football, from grassroots all the way to an elite 'farmhouse' like La Masia. The main idea is to let them express themselves in ways in which they're most comfortable and then the coaches will do their best to nourish their strengths, improve on their weaknesses and, above all, let them play – something important that Mortezaie has been very vocal about in our discussion. Yes, Barcelona have different training blocks and sessions that focus on developing all sorts of different profile traits, but the key is to 'let them play'. They're children, after all.

But there's one more aspect we have to touch upon here that's unique to Lionel Messi the player and Lionel Messi the person, and that's special talent. Even though development isn't linear, the truth is that some children are inevitably more talented than others. So how does one approach bigger talents? Many young players with huge potential end up having average careers and many are late bloomers, achieving their very peak at later stages of their career. In that sense, it's difficult to successfully predict any youngster's development line.

Mortezaie ponders:

If you tell a big talent they're a very big talent and you approach them differently, how much have you actually helped them? There are so many things that need to go right at the same time, so maybe by approaching a big talent differently you're not helping them because you're giving them special attention they think they will get their whole life. And then when they are 15, 16, 17 or 18, they go to a club where everybody is like that. And all of a sudden they don't get that special attention anymore. So instead of telling them they're a big talent, rather focus on how they can use that exceptional skill to get better and ensure their team is better. It's about creating mini challenges for them all the time.

I absolutely love the last part regarding 'mini challenges'. How can you take your god-given talent and put it to even better use to help the team? You're obviously incredibly good at X so why don't you try to complement it with Y or Z? Remember Messi's challenge to score more headed goals when he was really young?

Back in Argentina, his youth coach Carlos Marconi from Rosario, knowing Leo's love for chocolate cookies called *alfajores*, struck a deal with the kid, saying that he would get a cookie for every goal he scored. But since it wasn't unusual for Messi to score four or five goals per match, Marconi quickly realised he was running out of cookies. So in a cheeky attempt to turn the tide back in his favour, he altered the rules of the game, saying Messi would now get two cookies per goal but the trick was that only headers counted. Messi was obviously never tall and powerful so scoring headers was very difficult. But he was incredibly creative and used other skills in his arsenal to beat the challenge. He would dribble to the goalkeeper, getting past all the defenders on his way, beat the goalie too and then juggle the ball in the air right in front of the goal before scoring with his head. Along the way throughout his career, his talent would be posed with different challenges all the time, the first of which was the positional change.

Andy West recalled during our discussion on Leo:

> When he was a kid – and obviously children's football is less rigorously organised tactically, so [he] will have had the freedom then to do what he wanted – he played as the *enganche*, the traditional No.10. That was his role within the structure – to play the way he wanted. But he was also very small and very slender in his early Barcelona days.

No.10s are players that are granted positional freedom and often decreased defensive responsibility – a perfect combination for someone of Messi's traits. But as he rose through the ranks, football became more complex but also more structured and rigid. One player deviating from the plan was putting the whole collective at risk but, luckily, such is the extent of Leo's talent that it mattered very little.

The academy Messi is very similar to the one we saw in the early stages of his first-team journey at Barcelona but he was also very raw. Watching him play, even if only through clips and limited footage, is dazzling. That version of Messi was just unrestrained talent and raw skill. The way he changed directions at full speed or swapped between controlling the ball with his right or his left foot was simply outrageous. The young Messi would break defenders' ankles if they tried to mimic his movement but he also over-relied on it, sometimes dribbling when he should have passed and vice versa.

West explains:

By watching his early youth games, you can see it's Messi, but he doesn't have the awareness he now has. He runs with his head down, he runs into dead ends, doesn't have that pause to take a step, look up and take a look at the game around him. That was the thing that had to improve. And obviously it did, to a ridiculous degree.

This is certainly true. Messi's signature runs and control have become a staple over the years but while they were always present, they weren't exactly refined. He would often play either through the middle or, interestingly, down the left flank. So to suddenly change to the right wing to accommodate Ronaldinho, the star of Rijkaard's Barça, wasn't an easy task. This would ultimately mould Messi's profile even more.

As talented as he was, he still wasn't familiar with all the concepts that were key at Barcelona. As Samuel Marsden puts it: 'Messi was a mix of this Argentine street player who was able to mould and grasp the style and demands of Barcelona, also fairly early in his career.' It wasn't an instantaneous change, far from it. But from the very start he was learning, taking it all in and, most importantly, evolving.

From his very first game for the U14B team back in 2001, climbing the ladder through Barça's C and B teams, to his debut in the first team under Rijkaard, Messi was constantly improving and moulding his profile, both for his and the club's sake. Eventually, he became far too big to stay at the lower levels, even becoming 'a bit bored playing for the B team', as Sid Lowe told me. Everyone knew the time had come for him to step up.

So step up he did. This is his story.

Chapter 2

The Making of Lionel Messi

Trial by Fire

In the summer of 2003, Franklin 'Frank' Edmundo Rijkaard replaced Radomir Antić as the new coach of Barcelona. This, not unlike many of the more recent appointments over in Catalonia, was a knee-jerk reaction to what was going on around the club, both on and off the pitch. Antić, having only been in charge for 24 matches following the dismissal of Louis van Gaal, was promptly removed from the position as the new board came to power. Perhaps it was a cruel twist of fate for the Serbian gaffer, but a young and brimming Joan Laporta, fresh from his victorious presidential campaign, was eager to instil a coach of his own choosing. It was to be the start of a new era – and a new era had to begin with a new coach, regardless of whether the current one was, in fact, supposed to be exactly that in the first place.

But, interestingly, Rijkaard wasn't even Laporta's first choice. Actually, he wasn't even the second one either. Having failed to acquire either of Guus Hiddink or, ironically, Ronald Koeman, Laporta turned to Rijkaard who was, against all odds, backed by Johan Cruyff himself. That in itself was entertaining because Cruyff and Rijkaard went way back and, needless to say, had had a very turbulent history. But all of that was swept under the rug with the Dutchman appointed the new head coach for the 2003/04 season, officially his first one in charge. Considering Van Gaal had left the team in total disarray, having ended his tenure in 12th place before Antić somehow pulled them back to sixth with only 56 points to their name, there was nowhere for Rijkaard and his team to go but up.

However, everyone knew the climb, if there was ever going to be one at all, would be very difficult. And difficult it was indeed. Barcelona's quest for redemption got off to a very rocky start when Rijkaard's squad won just two out of their first seven matches, casting doubts left, right and centre. The then-board member Sandro Rosell lobbied to have the Dutchman replaced by Luiz Felipe Scolari but Laporta stuck to his guns, the same way he would put his trust into Pep Guardiola some years later, and it paid off.

Rijkaard was still struggling, of course. As a manager, he had a distinct idea of how football should be played. But, sadly, that hardly aligned with the squad he had at hand. By December, Barcelona already looked completely down and out, looking more likely to lose yet another coach than competing for the title. Having just been completely dismantled by Juande Ramos's Málaga, who put five goals past them while allowing just one, the Catalans were stranded in ninth place with the fans and the press calling for the coach's head. It didn't help that the home fans at Málaga's *La Rosaleda* were chanting 'A Segunda, a Segunda', quite enjoying the show that was unfolding before their eyes and, of course, pouring more oil on the fire that was starting to grow.

Sadly, Barça's struggles were far from over. Three days later, none other than Real Madrid would plunder a 2-1 victory at the Camp Nou as Carlos Queiroz's *Galácticos*, the reigning champions of Spain, would prove far too much for Rijkaard to handle – for now, at least. And the worst part yet? It was *Los Blancos'* first Camp Nou *Clásico* victory in two decades! For 20 years, this was a fortress for Barcelona against Real Madrid, the one place where the balance of power was maybe not as tilted in the Whites' favour. But even that was taken from them. In a rather similar fashion, January got off to a disastrous start too. Following another humiliating 3-0 defeat, this time against Racing, Barcelona had only two wins from nine matches in LaLiga and were languishing in 12th, 18 points behind then-league leaders Real Madrid.

But the moment of recovery was just around the corner, and in their darkest hour, with the coach's job very much on the line, Patrick Kluivert's goal at Ramón Sánchez-Pizjuán Stadium against Sevilla instilled hope once more. January was very much a time for changes, only now they would finally work in Barcelona's favour. With Ronaldinho already at the club from the summer of 2003, Rijkaard would also add Edgar Davids to the team and revert back to a more Cruyffian approach with a 4-3-3 formation and a slightly altered style of play. The added firepower of Davids worked quite well alongside his compatriot Phillip Cocu and also helped unlock a young Xavi Hernández to feed the front three with threading passes.

With performances vastly improved, results would soon follow too. Barcelona managed to string together a series of successful scalps, going 17 matches unbeaten before Celta Vigo brought them back to reality, ultimately preventing them from snatching the title from a rampaging Valencia. But that silver medal had the taste of gold considering the way the season had started for the Catalans. From 12th and with rock-bottom morale to second and a step away from the title was more than they could have hoped for.

But the best was yet to come. The following season would finally see Barcelona chase off the demons of their past and for the first time in five long years, the LaLiga crown would return to Catalonia and to the Camp Nou. But what no one knew at that point was that, despite the importance of that 2004/05 title, it wasn't the biggest turning point in the club's fortunes. That came in the form of a long-haired, skinny 17-year-old kid named Lionel Messi, who would make his debut under Rijkaard and soon take over the world. Of course, even though his name wouldn't make nearly as much noise as in the years to come, the young Argentine was already being heralded as an incredible talent back then. Everyone knew that kid was special, but hardly anyone could have predicted what came next.

On 16 November 2003, Messi made his debut for the first team at 16 years, 4 months and 23 days old, coming on as a substitute in the 75th minute during a friendly match against none other than José Mourinho's Porto. It didn't take 'La Pulga' ('The Flea') too long to captivate not only his team-mates and coach but also the opposition, with the Portuguese gaffer on the other side duly taking notes of a player that would terrorise his teams in the years to come.

From that moment on, Messi would regularly train with Barcelona B and the first team, eventually achieving his competitive debut on 6 March in Segunda División B for the former and 16 October in LaLiga for the latter. The second debut, and by far the more important, came in an away derby against Barcelona's bitter Catalan rivals Espanyol, in front of 34,400 fans in the stands. Leo replaced Deco in the 82nd minute, aged 17 years, 3 months and 22 days, and also wearing the No.30 shirt on his back.

Of course, 2004/05 was the season of his debut, but he would also remain a bit-part substitute player, registering only 77 minutes in nine matches for the first team, and also making another big debut in the UEFA Champions League, against Shakhtar Donetsk. It wasn't until 2005/06, the next most important year of Rijkaard's era, that Messi would finally start getting some continuity with the team. However, even with him gaining prominence with each passing day, it was far from smooth sailing for the Argentine magician.

These seasons were marked by big moments, such as his growing partnership with Ronaldinho or the first hat-trick in *El Clásico*, but also with major muscular problems as Messi struggled with injuries aplenty. One such problem prevented him from featuring in the Champions League Final against Arsenal. Even though he worked hard to regain fitness just in time for the big day, Rijkaard opted against including him in the squad, prompting Messi to not celebrate his team's victory in Paris. But sadly, as his development skyrocketed, Barcelona as a collective started to suffer more with each passing day. Rijkaard suddenly had an almost star-studded team but also one that increasingly lacked any cohesion, chemistry and, most importantly, work rate. The likes of Ronaldinho and Deco were sadly the main culprits despite at the same time still being the team's biggest stars. This, of course, would change very soon as both were on borrowed time. As was Rijkaard.

By the time 2007/08 rolled around, the Dutchman, and his team, were running on fumes, despite having players such as Andrés Iniesta, Ronaldinho, Lionel Messi and Xavi Hernández at his disposal, and with many others also at the peak of their powers. Interestingly, Guillem Balague recalls a story about Pep Guardiola facing Rijkaard's squad in a training match against Barcelona B. 'He [Pep] finally came to the conclusion that Barcelona needed a change [that day],' said Balague. 'He discovered Rijkaard smoking a cigarette … Ronaldinho was taken off after ten minutes, Deco was clearly tired and the reserve boys, still in the third division, were running the first team ragged.' Needless to say, Rijkaard's tenure was coming to an end and not a moment too soon.

But as bad as it was by the end, this era is perhaps unjustly remembered largely for the fall from grace. We often forget that this was the man to introduce Messi to the world, give him a debut and then guide him through the first tender years of his senior career. As a whole, Rijkaard managed Barça in 283 official matches, winning 167, drawing 64 and registering 52 defeats, with 544 goals scored and 254 conceded. This was good enough for a win percentage of 59 per cent and an average of 1.92 goals scored and 0.89 conceded per match, not to mention two LaLiga titles and a Champions League crown in an era when Barcelona didn't even dare to dream.

'Rijkaard. Just because at that spell of your career when you're younger, coaches and players have more of an impression on you. Rijkaard brought Barcelona back to relevance and he gave Messi his debut so he was an important coach for him,' said Sam Marsden when I asked him about Messi's most influential coaches. While putting Guardiola at the top of the list is the obvious choice, it's difficult to ignore – or rather we *shouldn't* ignore – Rijkaard in this conversation. After all, Leo himself was always full of praise for his first senior-team manager, even stating outright that Rijkaard is, truly, the most important coach he's ever had. Messi told Egyptian television channel MBC:

> All the coaches I had at first left me things, but I think the most important thing in my career was Rijkaard. If he had not decided to get me in the first team to train and play perhaps I'd never have reached the first team. I always said [Rijkaard] was, for me, a very important person because he trusted me. He made me play in the first team.

Without a shadow of a doubt, La Pulga's beginnings at Barcelona were far from plain sailing. From injuries, inconsistencies, doubts and heartbreaking moments, the first era of Messi's player development was a rocky one. But it was also a necessary step for him to take before he evolved into the player we know today, which brings us neatly to the point where we'll make our first real jump into the analytical waters of this book.

The narrative part of Leo's early years in Catalonia, as scintillating as it was, is a well-known one, but also one that only tells half the actual story. The tactical and statistical background, however, will complete the picture and answer some different questions. What kind of a player was Lionel Messi when he made his debut under Rijkaard? How did the Dutchman incorporate him into his tactics and how well did it work?

Let's find out.

The Mazy Winger

The difference between Messi in the early years of his career and the Messi we know today is simply staggering. Of course, players change over time, and the very best ones adapt their styles of play depending on the needs of the team, the specific tactics for their era and their own skill set. But with Messi, his development was far from linear. Sure, practically anyone could tell he had talent even from the smallest of samples, but the surprise came in the alarmingly high improvement rate and pure diversification of his profile. Not many mazy wingers end up becoming total footballers by the latter stages of their careers. Of course, most, if not all, would struggle to reach half of what Messi has achieved over the years. He's by far the clearest example of a generational talent. That phrase is thrown around far too often for players who are, admittedly, talented, but not to the point they could mark a whole generation of footballers. Apart from the likes of Kylian Mbappé and Erling Braut Håland, it's difficult to pinpoint any one of the current crop of high-potential youngsters who could stake a claim to that title. Messi and Cristiano Ronaldo, on the other hand, are the only ones to have really warranted it and solidified their spots in modern football's hall of fame.

But this was not always so. At the very beginning of his career, there were doubts over Leo's long-term development. We've seen that injuries and inconsistencies played a part but so did his profile. Nowadays, Messi's and Barça's DNA, as horrible and irrelevant as that term may be, are very much the same because even now, when he's no longer their player, Messi is still synonymous with the club. He embodies their main principles, carries the style and represents the best of values that arise from La Masia. However, as we've mentioned already, the young and rash Messi making his debut under Frank Rijkaard was nowhere near the player he would eventually become. Álex Delmás puts it succinctly: 'If we compare Messi to his younger self, he's a much better player now in terms of understanding the play – he's more of a team player. In the beginning, he was more of an individualist. Now, he's a mix of the two.'

The key here is understanding that Messi would never forsake or sacrifice any of his qualities but would rather learn how to incorporate them into the demands of the team. Learning how to play with others and involving others into play would become crucial aspects of his development, both as an individual and as an important part of the collective. The very early stages of that development, however, were rather rough and raw. As a result of his preferred positions through the middle and to the left being occupied by big stars of the team such as Ronaldinho, Leo was 'relegated' to rotating on the right with Ludovic Giuly, another pacy winger

LIONEL MESSI'S PASS RECEPTION
FIRST ERA

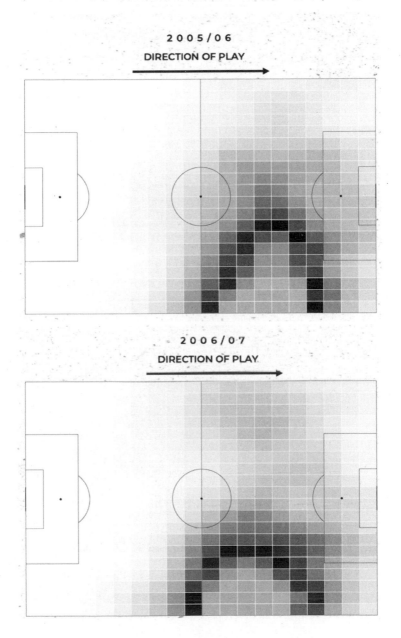

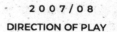

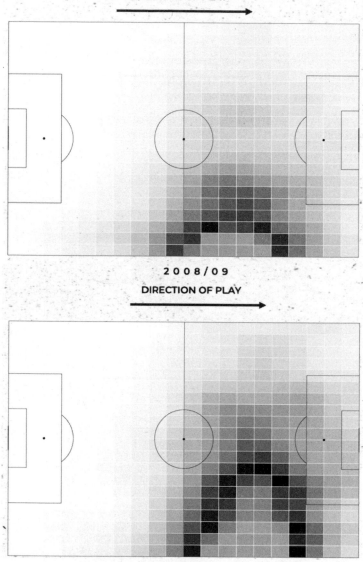

with an eye for goal who, at that time, was a safer and more common option for Rijkaard's Barcelona. When Messi did play, however, he was often seen far on the right wing, initially hugging the touchline and providing width and verticality to the team's tactics. We can read as much from these heatmaps, which will tell us more about his positioning and movement across the pitch.

Compared to the seasons that followed beyond 2008/09 and especially compared to the latter stages of his career, Messi's movement was predominantly focused on the wide areas, as expected. Of course, being a left-footer on the right side, it was more difficult for him to beat players towards the outside because that would mean going towards his weaker right foot. Instead, cutting inside towards his dominant foot made more sense and, with time, he developed the profile of an inverted winger. Somewhere along the line, he also managed to displace Giuly in the starting line-up, becoming a regular starter around the 2006/07 season.

Messi's talent made that possible, sure, but the differences in their profiles also played a big role. Despite his youth, Leo's incredible presence confused and dismantled opposition blocks and created space much more efficiently than anything Giuly could offer at the time. This is also where the first signs of future stardom started to appear, despite the likes of Ronaldinho still being in the team, albeit on borrowed time. But looking at some of Messi's prominent traits, we can confidently conclude that passing, at that point in his career, was mostly an irrelevant factor. Messi was used in short combinations and link-ups with an occasional through-ball but that was mostly it, as we'll see in the graphics, that outline his chance creation and overall assists. Reading this about Leo today sounds quite surreal but back then it was the reality – he was a tricky winger with hints of great one vs one ability but, other than that, there weren't any signs indicating that future elite playmaking or even goalscoring skills would ever be on the plate.

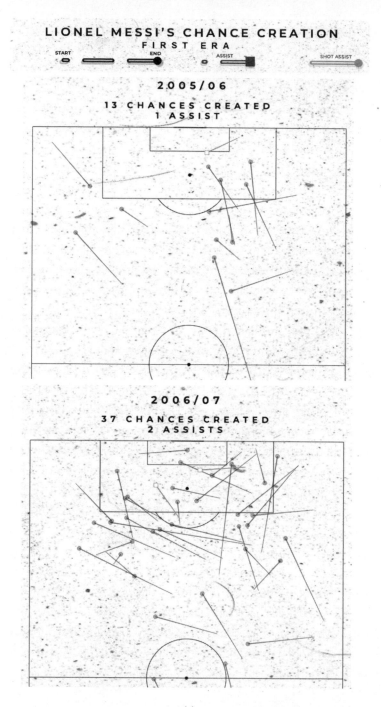

LIONEL MESSI'S CHANCE CREATION
FIRST ERA

START · END · ASSIST · SHOT ASSIST

2005/06

13 CHANCES CREATED
1 ASSIST

2006/07

37 CHANCES CREATED
2 ASSISTS

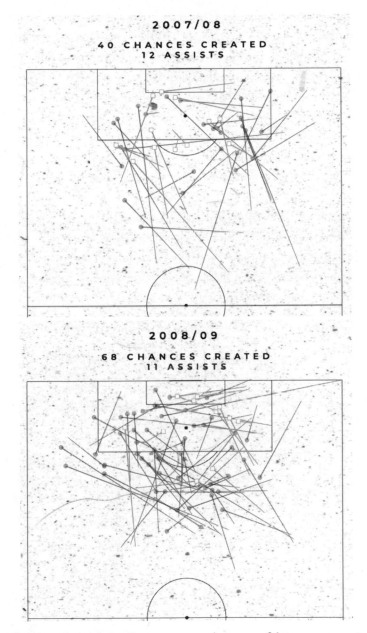

2007/08
40 CHANCES CREATED
12 ASSISTS

2008/09
68 CHANCES CREATED
11 ASSISTS

The graphics do tell a very good story of his progress in that department, however. Both the 2005/06 and 2006/07 campaigns were still shaky in terms of his passing tendencies but the jump is already clearly visible from one stage to the other. While the output in the former season is very low – 13 chances and one assist – the numbers are suddenly inflated in the latter with 37 chances and two assists. This is largely influenced by continuity. In his breakout seasons, Messi was plagued by muscular injuries and couldn't establish himself as a starter despite obvious signs of immense talent hiding underneath the raw exterior. But with more game time came more evidence that Barcelona's strongest XI had to include the little Argentine as well.

One key thing he held over the likes of Giuly was that unpredictability and pure one vs one ability on the wings. Yes, the Frenchman was a player in a rather similar mould, but nowhere near as electric as the youngster aiming to displace

LIONEL MESSI'S OPPOSITION HALF CARRY CLUSTERS
FIRST ERA

2005/06

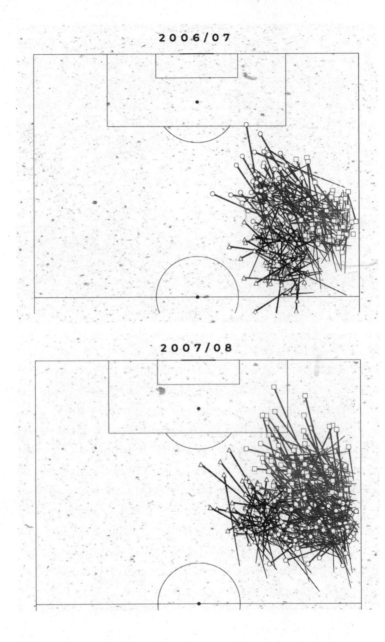

2006/07

2007/08

2008/09

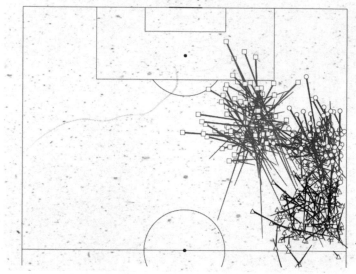

him for good. So, interestingly, when we talk about the early years of Messi's career, we can't really talk about passing or even about shooting and goals, but rather we have to focus on dribbles and carries. These graphics will tell us more about the development of his one vs one ability.

If there's one thing we can confidently say about the young Messi, it's the fact that he was brave in his dribbles and wanted to take players on – all the time. This, of course, may not be ideal for the team as a whole but it was very much a big part of his player profile back then. In his first start for Barcelona, Leo even completed more dribbles (11) than Ronaldinho (9), which was a sign of things to come. That season, he would average 7.4 completed dribbles for every 90 minutes played (from 9.77 attempts), which would continue growing over time despite a small dip in 2006/07, culminating in, so far, a career-high 8.4 per 90 minutes in 2007/08 (from 11.77 attempts).

Looking at the graphics showing his carries in the opposition half, we can see the wide starting location of all of those attempts. Of course, the growth in output itself is also clearly visible, but it's this tendency to hug the touchline and then dribble inwards that's very important to note here as it goes hand in hand with the whole theme of Messi the winger. 'When he played as a winger, he tried to play one-on-one far too often. Sometimes he won those duels but sometimes he would unnecessarily lose too many balls. He had to learn how to decide when to go one-on-one and when to avoid risk and combine with his team-mates instead,' explains Jordi Costa when talking about young Messi. And it's very much true. This is a trait many dribblers, young or even old, struggle with. There's a fine line between being the creative spark the team needs and overdoing it, and sometimes Leo would cross that line due to his inexperience and eagerness. Samuel Marsden rightfully calls this version of Leo a 'floppy-head teenager'. Although he was quick and tricky, teams learned how to beat and kick him around because of it, something that was true even in his academy days.

However, as much as he was still prolific in beating his man, Messi wasn't a big goalscoring threat, nor did he attack the box nearly as much. The graphics next depicting his penalty area entries will shed some light on that.

The numbers behind it also back up the whole narrative of a much lesser box presence compared to the years of success in that area that would soon follow. Messi averaged only 6.26, 5.39 and 5.54 touches in the box per 90 minutes in the depicted three seasons with Barcelona's first team under Rijkaard.

A very similar thing can be seen in his penalty-box entries with the ball. Most of those entrances are from the right flank and, subsequently, follow the same approach. When receiving possession, his first instinct was always to dribble past the marker in his immediate vicinity and then, if he somehow

LIONEL MESSI'S OPEN PLAY PENALTY BOX ENTRIES
FIRST ERA

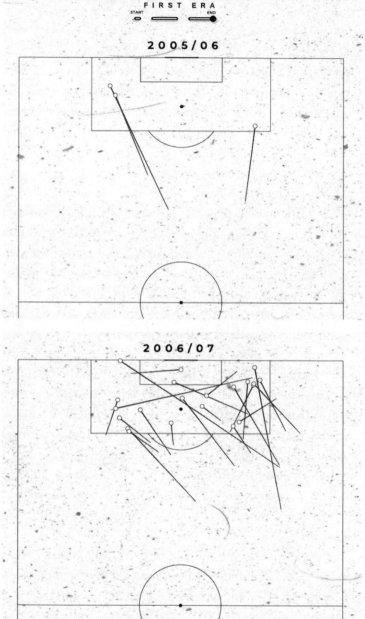

2005/06

2006/07

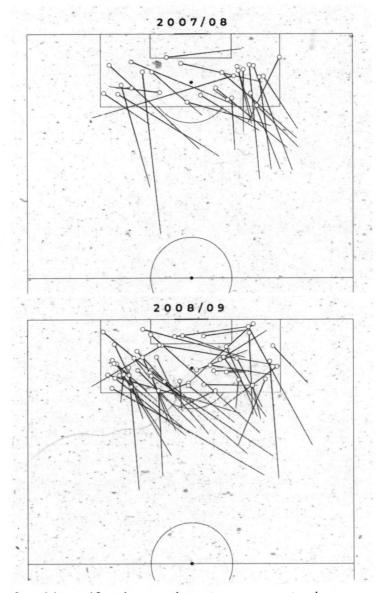

found himself with a good scoring opportunity, have a go for goal.

And this brings us to probably the most important aspect of Messi's player profile, or rather the aspect that would soon come to best describe him as a player: shooting technique and goalscoring prowess. Needless to say, his early years portrayed a player who was a far cry from the one he would eventually become and it was painfully obvious in terms of his shot locations and the pure quality of those attempts. We can see more in the clusters that depicts his shots and goals.

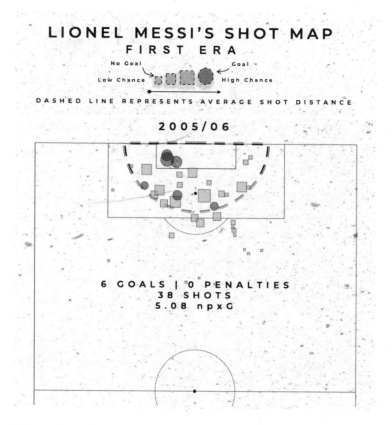

The rather glaring issue, especially in the first two seasons analysed, is the low quality of most of his shots. But even with that taken into consideration, his return was still quite impressive. Leo managed six and 14 goals in those two seasons, respectively, which is a great return overall for such a young and raw talent. Similarly, totals of 5.08 npxG (non-penalty

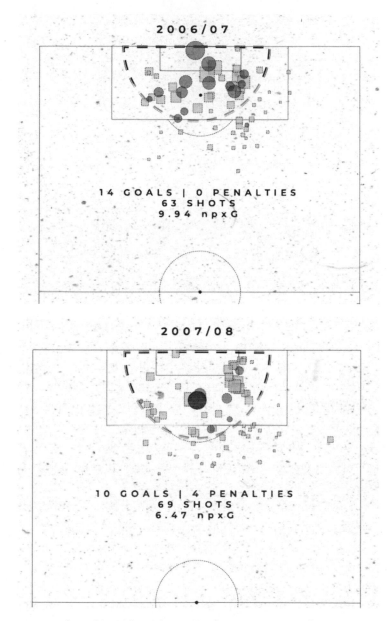

2006/07

14 GOALS | 0 PENALTIES
63 SHOTS
9.94 npxG

2007/08

10 GOALS | 4 PENALTIES
69 SHOTS
6.47 npxG

expected goals) and 9.94 npxG, showing overperformance in that department, suggest he was an acute finisher despite far from ideal shot locations and decision-making in the final

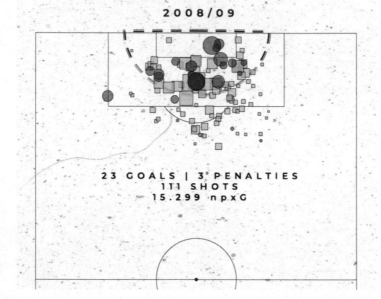

third. This is best seen in the lack of central shots, especially in the first two seasons, as Messi would take aim from the corners after cutting in from the right. Of course, that directly correlates with his initial positioning out wide, which gave him only one real way to enter the penalty area in the first place, as we've seen in the previous graphics. That resulted in very low xG per shot values too, amounting to 0.139 per shot from open play in 2005/06, 0.148 in 2006/07 and 0.081 in 2007/08.

A big leap in output happened around 2008/09 and the arrival of Pep Guardiola. Of course, even bigger changes were just around the corner, but this is where Messi was starting to hit his stride with 23 goals, 111 shots and 15.299 npxG, all of which were career highs for him at the time. In that season, he crucially added more shots from central positions, as opposed to heavily relying on angled attempts from the corners of the box, which significantly increased his chances and positively impacted the final tally of goals.

Now that we know a thing or two about his player profile in the Rijkaard era, let's see what that looked like on the pitch and within Barcelona's tactics at the time.

The drawing board

At this point in his career, Messi was very much still in development. Yes, his technical quality was through the roof but the rest of the repertoire was yet to come. This is especially true when it comes to his passing abilities but also concerns some fundamentals of how and when to move and also how and when to shoot. We've seen in the data and the visualisations that he often shot from less than ideal positions, while also attacking the box at very similar angles most of the time. Of course, this would improve drastically over the years, even at a surprising rate too, but in the first couple of seasons, the fact that Leo was a raw and unfinished product was clear for everyone to see. That, however, is not to say that he wasn't effective at what he did. There's a reason why Rijkaard, despite initially lacking trust in the youngster, slowly but surely phased Giuly out of the squad, replacing him with a teenager.

The next four sequences of play ranging from 2005 to 2008 will show us some of the classic Messi moments that best describe his profile at the time. Being the volume and deadly dribbler he was, it isn't exactly a surprise that *this* was his main weapon that made him stand out from the crowd.

Probably the best place to start, as ever, is the very beginning. The moment the world truly got to know Messi and also the moment when it fell in love with him was the annual Gamper Trophy tournament way back in 2005 when the Catalans faced Juventus. That was the match that also made Rijkaard realise the kid was going places, but his future would definitely be with Barça.

'They [Juventus players] were aggressive. And to see Messi put [Patrick] Vieira and [Pavel] Nedvěd on their ar**s and selling them dummies, it was hilarious and the crowd loved it. And that was the day Rijkaard knew he couldn't let Messi go on loan, he had to start using him,' Hunter told me, explaining what had happened that summer at the Camp Nou. Barcelona would end up losing the match after a penalty shoot-out went the *Bianconeri*'s way, but Leo himself would show everyone his worth and then some. The next graphic depicts one of his many great moments from the match, while also highlighting what he was all about back then.

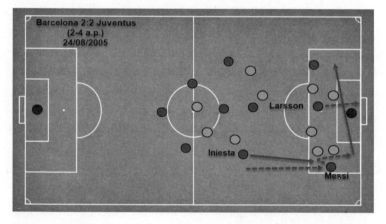

It's actually Iniesta who starts the attack as Barcelona are ripping Juventus apart in an attacking transition. The first thing to note here is the sheer pace young Messi possessed. He may not have been the fastest around but at that time he had more than just decent top speed at his disposal. The young Argentine starts his run from around the halfway line and receives a lovely pass from Iniesta just inside the opposition's box. It's there that he sends both Fabio Cannavaro and Gianluca Pessotto back to Italy with a cheeky feint before deploying a good, if slightly mishit, pass towards a marauding Henrik Larsson inside the six-yard box. The Swede sadly fails to convert and just misses the ball, allowing Juventus to eventually recover. But in a single sequence we saw Messi's pace, dribbling and even passing in action, signalling things to come in the near future.

Leo the young talent was gone, promptly replaced by Leo the future superstar. The crowd also went wild, chanting 'Messssi, Messsssi' immediately following the action. It's also important to remember that Leo never cared that he was facing the likes of Cannavaro, Nedvěd, Vieira, Giorgio Chiellini, Mauro Camoranesi, Alessandro Del Piero and Zlatan Ibrahimović. He never cared that they were bigger and stronger than him, completely shattering what old-fashioned belief Rijkaard had held back then.

Not long after that came *El Clásico* of November 2005, one that would be marked by Ronaldinho's brilliance and the famous applause from the Madrid crowd in the heart of the Santiago Bernabéu Stadium. But even though most talk was about the Brazilian's performance that night, and rightfully so, Messi was silently having an incredible match as well. At that time, it wasn't exactly the norm to play him as much, especially in away matches. So for him to feature against Real Madrid of all teams and even play as well as he did was extraordinary, in his *El Clásico* debut no less.

Hunter remembers, heaping praise on the young Argentine:

> He [Messi] is still very junior in his development. And because Ronaldinho scores those two amazing goals, everybody forgets how f*****g brilliant Messi was. Just like in the Juventus friendly, he played like the pitch was his own, the ball was his own. Being smaller than the Madrid guys didn't bother him at all. He was always looking to set up Ronaldinho and [Samuel] Eto'o, being unselfish.

So we'll revisit that match against Real Madrid with the following attacking sequence.

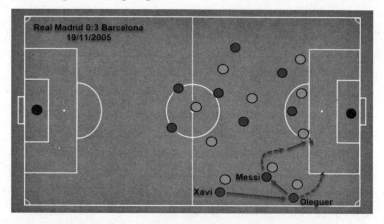

Again, the play shows Messi's most prominent traits but also some of his flaws at the time. Here, Xavi, Oleguer Presas and Messi combine on the right after a throw-in in the opposition's half. Leo receives the ball just at the entrance to the right half-space, beats his immediate marker almost effortlessly and then proceeds to cut inside towards the penalty area. However, although he has other options in Eto'o and Ronaldinho on the other side, he opts to shoot despite the defenders blocking his way forward. As a result, Real Madrid emerge unscathed from this promising sequence. Although over the years Messi would perfect his technique and score goals aplenty from this exact type of movement and positioning, at that time he was still learning how to decide when and from where to have a go.

This also takes us back to his shot maps from the Rijkaard era where we saw he would mostly enter the box from the right and register attempts from the edge of the penalty area rather than from central positions. Still, that didn't take away from the brilliant performance he gave that day, as Hunter explains, 'He was phenomenal that day. We were already talking about somebody who had the potential to be the club's all-time great, you could see that already.'

Ronaldinho may have received the mythical applause but Messi was ramping up to earn his own. It would, however, take some time for him to fully develop his arsenal. In 2008, Barcelona faced Osasuna and barely managed to scrape past them in a narrow 1-0 victory, hugely thanks to Xavi's late winner. But Messi was being Messi, albeit with hints of some immaturity still. In the sequence that follows, we see him go on a fairly standard run that sadly doesn't end in a goal.

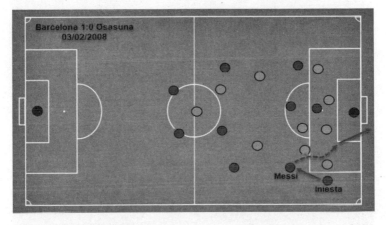

Leo receives the ball from Iniesta just around the edge of the penalty area to the right. Immediately after that, he slaloms through two Osasuna defenders, only to arrive just outside the six-yard box. Unfortunately, such was the angle of the entrance that he positioned himself on his right foot instead of the dominant left. While he *can* and *would* still score goals with his right, it would never be as proficient as his left. This results in Messi missing the target completely despite beating multiple markers relatively close to the opposition's goal. This, needless to say, was a suboptimal position to shoot from, both generally speaking and for him personally. Even if the shot had been on target, the angle wouldn't have allowed him to thread the ball past all the bodies that were soon in front of him. The goalkeeper blocked the near corner while the defender in his immediate vicinity could do the same with the far corner.

A shot from there resulting in a goal would have been difficult, even for Messi, but in the years to come he would learn to judge these situations much better, even preferring to pass over shooting when he deemed it the better option. One instance where the marauding dribbles would result in a magnificent goal, however, happened back in 2007 against Getafe. This goal, closely resembling that of the late Diego Armando Maradona's 'Goal of the Century' against England in 1986, would enter Barcelona folklore and would eventually be proclaimed Messi's best one ever – and rightfully so.

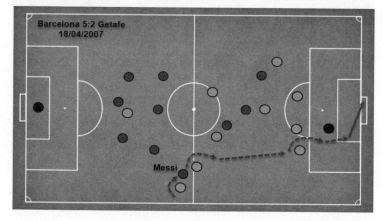

The sequence starts with the Argentine in Barcelona's half of the pitch but would end with the ball in the opposition's net. On his incredible run down the pitch, Messi would proceed to beat multiple players and the goalkeeper to slot the ball home, prompting the crowd – and commentators across the globe – to explode. Interestingly, he would almost replicate this attempt against Athletic Club years later, showing just how outstanding a dribbler he is. But between 2005 and 2008, that was the most impressive trait in his arsenal; not the only one, for sure, but the one that stood out the most. Rijkaard would learn how to properly wield it over time but incorporating Messi into his tactics wasn't as simple or as straightforward as it may seem.

Next, we'll explore some of Barcelona's most common set-ups during the Dutchman's reign and see just what role Messi played within them.

Rijkaard's Barça

Barcelona's revolution under Rijkaard started in 2003/04, and along with the Dutchman replacing Antić and Van Gaal, they also introduced a new repertoire of promising and talented players to the fans. Interestingly, unlike modern times, Barcelona's reinforcements of old didn't cost fortunes to secure – partly, of course, due to the state of the market today being out of control, and partly because of much better investment by the board back then. By far the biggest and most important addition, however, was that of the Brazilian World Cup winner Ronaldinho. The soon-to-be hero was brought in for the sum of €30m – pocket change in today's money – and unveiled in front of 20,000 *Culés* at the Camp Nou as the saviour to usher them into a better future.

But Ronaldinho wasn't the only signing that year, nor the only influential figure that would help Barça climb out of the doldrums. In addition to his signature, Laporta and Rijkaard also secured Ricardo Quaresma from Sporting CP, Rafael Márquez from Monaco and Turkish goalkeeper Rüştü Reçber from Fenerbahçe S.K. But change also often requires sacrifice, so the likes of Patrik Andersson, Philippe Christanval, Geovanni, Fábio Rochemback and even Juan Román Riquelme left the club, either on loan or permanently, to reduce the wage bill and free up some non-EU spots at the club.

Even with all those deals going through, the real change and palpable success wouldn't come before the arrivals of Samuel

Eto'o, Deco, Henrik Larsson, Juliano Belletti, Edmílson and Ludovic Giuly. The team that would eventually mark an era was starting to form, but Rijkaard's first months at the club were very difficult to say the least. The system and tactics he deployed early on in his tenure were a far cry from what they would eventually become. And yes, while we mostly associate his reign with the traditional Cruyffian 4-3-3 structure, Rijkaard wouldn't revert back to it until January 2004 and the addition of Edgar Davids on loan from Juventus.

The Dutchman's formation could be described as variations of 3-4-3, 4-2-3-1 and even at times a 4-4-2 with a double pivot down the middle channels. The real 4-3-3 was established with Davids partnering Cocu and Xavi in a midfield trident that would finally unlock their potential. However, that trio wouldn't last as both Dutchmen were quickly replaced by Deco and Mark van Bommel, arriving in 2004/05 and 2005/06, respectively. By that year, the foundations were already set, with a certain Lionel Messi registering appearances off the bench.

The diminutive Argentine talent would tally 18 LaLiga appearances for Barcelona that season, but the problem La Pulga faced at the very beginning of his journey under Rijkaard was the lack of trust. Many, including Leo himself, herald the Dutchman as a hugely important figure in the development of his player profile, and rightly so. However, that's not nearly the whole story. When he was first breaking out from La Masia, Messi struggled to convince his coach that he was indeed ready for the first team, so much so that there were initial conversations about a potential loan deal to Rangers. Alex McLeish was the manager of the Ibrox club at that time when talks between the clubs started about Messi. Intriguingly, it was McLeish's son Jon who saw Messi on *Football Manager* and kept telling his dad, 'Lionel Messi is going to be the best player in the world.' Of course, little did McLeish know that would

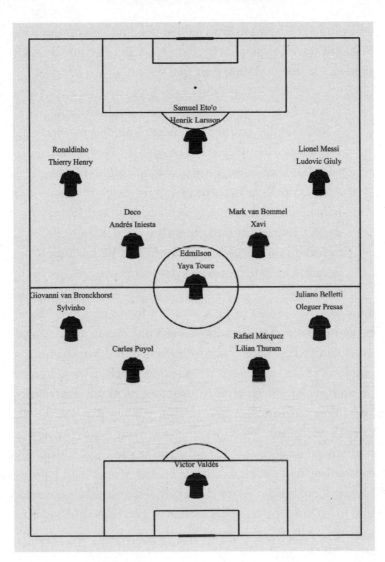

Samuel Eto'o
Henrik Larsson

Ronaldinho
Thierry Henry

Lionel Messi
Ludovic Giuly

Deco
Andrés Iniesta

Mark van Bommel
Xavi

Edmílson
Yaya Toure

Giovanni van Bronckhorst
Sylvinho

Juliano Belletti
Oleguer Presas

Carles Puyol

Rafael Márquez
Lilian Thuram

Víctor Valdés

indeed turn out to be true. Rangers did make the inquiry in the end but nothing came to be.

However, the whole situation is intriguing because Rijkaard himself was considering it. Graham Hunter explained to me that it was mostly due to Messi's physique; yes, he was talented beyond measure but also tiny, and being the mould of player and subsequently coach who valued both technique and size, Rijkaard was not completely sold on diminutive players such as Messi or Iniesta. Hunter argues:

> Rijkaard was being told by a B team coach: 'This kid is ready, this kid is ready,' but he was a product of what he'd learned as a player at Ajax and the Netherlands and the era he came through. Think about his size or attitude. Rijkaard's idea was very much that you needed to be big and tough and athletic and able to defend yourself as well. But also you'd have to be technical too. So in Messi and Iniesta he saw little guys and he didn't immediately trust them.

This would continue to be a problem for Iniesta, but Messi, being head and shoulders above everyone else in all technical drills and ability, made Rijkaard turn his head and change his opinion. That's when we started seeing much more of Leo in the starting XI. However, this insistence on physical attributes and improved fitness would still play a big part in Messi's early development. We know that recurring injuries plagued the Argentine during Rijkaard's era at the club, ultimately preventing him from featuring in the iconic Champions League Final against Arsenal. But all of that would eventually lead to creating the very best version of Leo the world had ever seen, under Pep Guardiola. However, it's crucial that Pep isn't given all the credit for the making of arguably the greatest player of all time.

In that period, Barcelona had already realised that Messi was an incredible asset and would continue to be for years to come. However, he was also a very fragile asset too. Marc Ingla, the club's director of sport back then, decided they needed to protect the Argentine at all costs, learning from the mistakes of the past. And that's where the colossal changes for Leo started to happen, as Hunter explains:

> He [Marc Ingla] insisted on a complete change of diet – not the Argentinian diet of nothing but red meat and potatoes – and he insisted that there was a dietician involved who predominantly introduced fish and vegetables. So they changed his diet and asked him to look at his stretching and assigned a physical coach to him called [Juanjo] Brau.

We all know the story of hormone injections but a change in Messi's approach to training, diet and rest were crucial in helping him reach and sustain the godly form that was soon to be revealed. And that ultimately allowed Guardiola to get the best out of Leo too.

Hunter continues:

> He [Brau] became attached to Messi and everything changed. Not just the physical preparation but also how he warmed down after games, the balance of gym and fieldwork, what kind of rest he was getting, what kind of a physio and massage he was getting – they overhauled all of that. That meant that by the time Guardiola was taking over, they were getting the best version of Messi in terms of physique and athleticism, minimising the risk of injury but also to have him perform at his most powerful and most consistent level.

This is very important to understand because none of the tactical and profile evolution we would see from Messi in the years to come would have been possible without first setting the foundations properly.

But this isn't Rijkaard's only contribution to Leo's development. Yes, there was a lack of trust present at the beginning, but the Argentine's performances couldn't be ignored and soon he would completely displace Giuly in the line-up, starting far more regularly on that right but also left flank. The next graphic tells us more about the structure he was played in at that time.

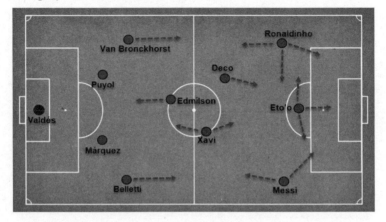

Rijkaard's Barcelona were very insistent on possession, as is the traditional Barça way. That meant having secure ball-playing centre-backs in Carles Puyol and Rafael Márquez. Recycling possession and retaining the ball were important aspects that would be refined in the years following the Dutchman's sacking but it was during his tenure that Barcelona would once again lay the foundations for things to come.

The backline was aggressive both on and off the ball and would regularly receive help from the central midfielders. Rijkaard often played with two deeper midfielders, one with more freedom to go forward. Before the emergence of Sergio Busquets's pivot profile, Barcelona had the likes of Edmílson and Yaya Touré perform that role in a slightly different manner. The defensive midfielder was exactly that, dropping very deep and protecting the backline off the ball and helping the team transition into the middle third on it. But it wasn't just Edmílson that would regularly drop to connect the thirds in the first phase of the attack. As we'll soon see, the movement of the midfielders depended on the side Barcelona wanted to achieve progression from. Advancing down the left would often see Edmílson drop deeper, while advancing through the right activated Xavi's drop closer to the backline.

Deco, on the other hand, was then given the freedom to join the attack alongside a deadly trident in Ronaldinho, Eto'o and, of course, Messi. Before Leo, we saw Giuly regularly start on that right flank but the Frenchman would offer a slightly different profile from the one the Argentine would soon develop.

'When he [Messi] first appeared for Barcelona's first team with Rijkaard on the bench as coach, he played as a right-winger and he always stayed wide until there was an opportunity to go on goal. At that moment, the player with freedom of movement was, of course, Ronaldinho and not Messi,' Jordi Costa told me about Leo's role. And this was largely true because the Brazilian was the star of the team and he was granted the freedom to do whatever he wanted or deemed necessary in any given situation.

That being said, however, both Ronaldinho and Messi shared some similar traits in their roles within Rijkaard's system. Both were wingers, yes, but they would drop deeper, stay wide or invert depending on the other's movement. With Ronaldinho often being tasked with progression down the left, either via his incredible dribbling or passing skills, Messi would often hug the touchline and attempt to stretch the pitch, using his gravity to attract defenders. If the Brazilian was wide, however, Messi had the freedom to invert and occupy far more central positions. This played a big part in dictating Barcelona's build-up phase as well. You can see a very basic but also a regular sequence in the following tactics board.

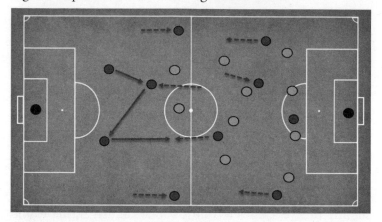

I've already touched upon the movement of the midfielders and exactly that can be seen here. Edmílson would regularly drop to create a numerical superiority against a very predominant 4-4-2 defensive approach of their opposition and then recycle the ball until a gap could be exploited. In this instance, the defensive midfielder lays it off to the other centre-back and from there the defender would look for Xavi or Mark van Bommel, who was the other midfielder with regular appearances in Rijkaard's era, to progress the play.

This is also where it's important to talk about Ronaldinho and Messi once more. Their presence was very significant in the build-up phase as it allowed Barcelona's main creators and progressors to start attacks from deep. We can look at their in-possession structure under Rijkaard in more detail by observing the pass map from a match against Deportivo La Coruña back in 2007. There are several aspects we should make note of when analysing the graphic. Firstly, starting with the backline, we can see how both centre-backs are heavily involved and are tasked with heavy ball recycling in the first phase of build-up.

But just as they're tasked with initial progression, Xavi and Edmílson are the midfielders closest to them. Prior to Sergio Busquets's emergence, Edmílson was a somewhat different type of pivot within Barcelona's tactics. He was certainly good on the ball and could drop deep to assist the build-up, but we can see that he was nowhere near as involved or influential as his successor would eventually become. Xavi, on the other hand, was, and so was Iniesta when he eventually broke through into the team. Both midfielders were key to unlocking the side's potential and set up the extremely prolific forward line.

But due to Ronaldinho's presence, Rijkaard's Barcelona were heavily tilted towards the left side of the pitch. The Brazilian's biggest connections were Van Bronckhorst just behind him and Eto'o just ahead, with Iniesta drifting outward at times as well. Together, and with the midfield's support and Leo's counterweight on the other side, they formed the major brunt of Barcelona's attacking prowess.

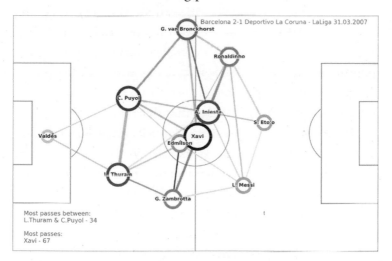

Barcelona 2-1 Deportivo La Coruna - LaLiga 31.03.2007

Most passes between:
L.Thuram & C.Puyol - 34

Most passes:
Xavi - 67

Messi was slightly different and, at that time, not as important as his star team-mate on the opposite flank. Of course, this was already starting to change, but it would take a little longer to fully come to fruition. Interestingly, Messi and Ronaldinho formed a great partnership too, which can also be seen from the pass map. With both of them boasting incredible close control and dribbling, they had the ability to beat markers and conquer space like very few team-mates or opponents could. And it's exactly that trait that would make Rijkaard's Barcelona very potent in transitions too. One only has to think back to Ronaldinho's legendary match against Real Madrid at the Santiago Bernabéu Stadium when he received a standing ovation from *Los Blancos'* fans – a very uncommon gesture to this day. The Brazilian's marauding runs still haunt the Whites' dreams as the combination of pace, power and technique remain almost unmatched even more than a decade later.

Barcelona's frontline was very much about pace and power, as much as it boasted an abundance of technique too. Ronaldinho was a brute with elegance, being able to outmuscle defenders as well as humiliate them with tricks. Eto'o was extremely versatile, while being a world-class goalscorer, and Messi's arsenal was an ever-expanding one that would soon transition into a profile of a complete forward. Hitting the opposition on the break, therefore, was an incredibly potent weapon in Rijkaard's arsenal, helped no end by a midfield capable of supplying ample ammunition.

In that match against Real Madrid, one of Ronaldinho's goals came after a failed cross into the box by the hosts. The ball is quickly cleared and then sent towards Ronaldinho, who was hugging the touchline around the halfway line.

And then in the blink of an eye, in a run that's still as remarkable all these years later, Ronaldinho beats two defenders before slamming the ball past a helpless Iker Casillas. It's pretty interesting to note the movement of the other forwards in this instance too. Barcelona didn't have real wingers at that time since both Ronaldinho and Messi liked to cut in centrally, but

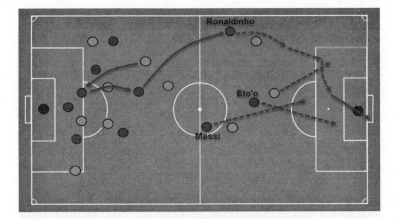

they never lacked pace either. Both Eto'o and Messi had no trouble following up on the attack. Ronaldinho himself and his Cameroonian team-mate were often positioned around the halfway line of the pitch for that very purpose too, while the rest of the team defended in a mid-to-low block.

Leo was much more active defensively, as we'll soon discuss, but would easily join the other two forwards in an attacking transition, even covering the whole pitch relatively quickly, as in the earlier example against Real Madrid. The movement of Eto'o is quite interesting because he was a very willing runner and extremely hard-working, also reasons Guardiola decided to stick with him for a while following his appointment after Rijkaard. Since Messi and Ronaldinho weren't traditional wingers but were granted a certain dose of free movement, Eto'o often found himself reacting to their positioning, which further displayed his quality. If Messi was in a more central position attacking the box, Eto'o would easily drift out wide to either combine with the full-back or just to fill the void left by the Argentine. This versatility and spatial awareness were crucial to making Barcelona's attack as potent as it was back then. But when we discuss versatility, we simply have to touch upon their direct approach to attacking football.

Nowadays, it's very unusual to see Barcelona practise direct or transitional styles of play, but under Rijkaard this wasn't as frowned upon. Yes, they were a possession-based team, but with a lot of pace down the flanks through Messi, a drifting Eto'o and a very physically dominant Ronaldinho, the long-ball approach wasn't that uncommon. If we take the Champions League Final against Arsenal as an example, one of the main ways Barcelona aimed to attack the London side was through sharp diagonal balls from Márquez to either Eto'o on the left or Giuly on the right. Messi, remember, wasn't deemed fit enough by Rijkaard to participate. It's actually Ronaldinho's ability to shield the ball and control it with his back to goal that ultimately made this a viable approach too. The Brazilian's incredible mix of brute strength and technique made him a very difficult player to pin down and stop so Barcelona naturally made use of that by diversifying their attacking schemes.

A very similar notion of diversity and versatility was also present in their settled phase of possession in the final third. Rijkaard was insistent on dominating the ball, and his team was used to controlling matches within the opposition's half of the pitch. And, of course, movement plays a crucial part there too. Similarly to how they operate nowadays, defensive midfielders would stay closer to the centre-back duo for both cover and ball retention, while the other two midfielders joined the attack or plugged holes out wide. Deco was the more aggressive of the two, as would Iniesta become in due course, while Xavi dictated matches from a deeper position and threaded passes to the forwards from the right side.

Messi and Ronaldinho's movement is once again extremely interesting here. They both attacked the box and would soon become a lethal tandem with complementary movement. Just as before, both would have a wider starting position but preferred to cut inside towards the penalty area. Both, too,

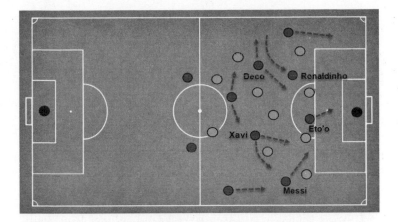

excelled in one vs one duels and thrived when isolated with their markers, which would soon become a priority for other teams to avoid. Although Rijkaard preferred the newcomer Giuly over the La Masia talent in the early stages of his tenure, that changed rather quickly too. While the Frenchman was a very direct and tricky winger who could do the work on the right, he didn't have Leo's ability to progress the ball and disrupt opposition blocks from the right half-space.

Soon, Messi was doing everything Giuly could do and much, much more as he became a mainstay in the line-up, completely displacing his direct competition for the spot. But at this point in Leo's career, it's also very important to talk about pressing and his work off the ball. Since Ronaldinho was the star of the team and the player given the freedom to roam the pitch but also the freedom from too much defensive responsibility, Messi had to press and defend harder to compensate.

Rijkaard told *The Guardian* back in 2006:

> Ronaldinho is the only one who has a free role. He normally starts in midfield but then becomes more of an attacker as the game progresses. Because he

doesn't do any defensive work I want the rest of the team to balance that. So when he leaves his flank it is important that the other three midfielders move in that direction, or we can end up with a lot of open space for our opponents to attack if we lose the ball.

This is also where that versatility in movement comes into play again. We've already mentioned how the midfielders will often cover the flanks even in the attacking phase and the same is true off the ball. To prevent Van Bronckhorst from being isolated and burned on the break, Edmílson, Van Bommel or even Deco would shift over to cover that area and shut down the vast acres of space that would otherwise be available to the opposition.

Out of possession, Barcelona aimed to control the middle of the pitch by shutting down central channels of progression for the opposition. Their trademark 4-3-3 would transform into a variation of a narrow 4-2-2-2 and a 4-1-2-1-2. Ronaldinho and Eto'o would still be the furthest players up the pitch to lead the break and Messi often tucked in behind them to join the attack should the opportunity present itself.

Rijkaard himself admitted to being heavily influenced by the Italian style that predominantly focused on solid defensive organisation. He told *The Guardian* in 2006:

> Someone said that my coaching is a combination of Milan's defensive discipline and the Dutch propensity for attacking football and I think that is a fair description. I try to merge the two schools of thought. There is a part of football I would describe as 'serious' and one part I would describe as more 'playful'.

While the signature pressing schemes wouldn't come along until Guardiola's arrival, Rijkaard's Barcelona were already implementing bits and pieces of it years before. The Catalan giants were very aggressive off the ball and deployed a high man-marking press that aimed to win the ball close to the opposition's box.

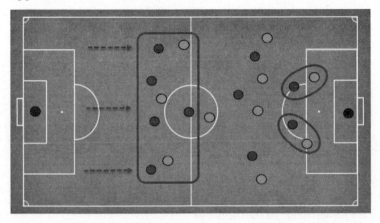

There are a couple of important aspects we have to identify here. Firstly, the height of the defensive line had increased significantly. Barcelona would look to make the pitch smaller by pushing up towards the opposition's half and essentially limiting their operating area. However, since that was a risky approach, especially against pacy forwards who would love nothing more than to exploit all the space in behind, an appropriate cover needed to be in place. This is why the defensive midfielder would often stay close to the backline, either man-marking the opposition's player between the lines or even dropping so deep that it appeared more like a five-man defence.

The full-backs were often deeper as well, depending on the positioning of the opposition wingers. However, they could push up to press if Barcelona were in danger of a numerical inferiority. Two forwards, usually Ronaldinho and Eto'o, would press the centre-backs, while the midfield had the difficult task of covering a lot of ground across the middle third of the pitch. This is where at times they were exposed, as good teams could still play through them if the press wasn't coordinated well. Generally speaking, though, Rijkaard was praised for both his attacking and defensive tactics, while quality in both phases ensured domination and, ultimately, silverware.

However, by the end of Rijkaard's tenure, Barcelona were but a shadow of their former selves; stars on big wages living the life they never could before. It was a disaster waiting to happen – and happen it did. Rijkaard's final years were barren of any silverware and success, prompting the board to sack the man who had reinvigorated the club. In his place came an unknown quantity rising through the ranks of La Masia. Little did anyone know that he would bring about the most successful era of the club and with it the most successful version of Lionel Messi to date.

Chapter 3
Rebirth & Reinvention

A New Hope

You would be forgiven if you weren't feeling optimistic following the end of Frank Rijkaard's tenure as Barcelona coach. The last two seasons under the Dutch gaffer were a far cry from the 2005/06 campaign in which he achieved the double by winning the LaLiga trophy and the elusive Champions League crown. Those days were long gone and the Catalans needed something special to bring the magic back to the Camp Nou. Few would have put their money on the unproven Barcelona B coach being ready to step up; Joan Laporta's decision to put all his trust in Pep Guardiola would soon be vindicated, but to say that choosing him over José Mourinho raised some eyebrows would be a severe understatement. After all, Barcelona needed a proven commodity in the world of football – a winner who could give you results right here and right now, without too much risk. Pep, for all his success with the B team, was far from that prospect.

But Laporta trusted his gut. Within the span of a couple of years, Guardiola's Barcelona would already be viewed as one of the best around, and by the end of 28 May 2011, it would enter the footballing hall of fame. Naturally, looking at the struggles of the modern-day *Azulgranas*, and whether or not you followed the club ten years ago, this may or may not be a concept difficult to understand. After all, how could such a giant of the industry experience a drop of that magnitude? Sadly, there's no short or simple answer to that question apart from bad management. The fall from grace was very much a long process; a process consisting of one wrong decision at a time – a whole litany of them, in fact, as we'll see in more detail in the final chapters of this book.

But going back to the golden years of Barcelona under Pep, this too was a long process. No one could have predicted that what started on warm July afternoons in Scotland would eventually end in world domination – quite literally. Of course, the very beginnings were tough, as all beginnings usually are. Not many need reminding that Barcelona lost their opening match of the now almost legendary campaign 1-0 to Numancia and then went on to draw 1-1 with Racing Santander in front of the home crowd of the Camp Nou. That's only one point from a possible six and a far from ideal start to a brand-new era that was supposed to bring dominance and glory back to Catalonia. But that's exactly what would ultimately happen.

That Barça, 'Pep's Barça', would go on to win everything there was to win, including the hearts of many supporters; many old ones and undoubtedly even more new ones to come over the years. They would all soon start believing in whatever Guardiola was preaching at that time. And belief plays such an important part in the whole story – not least because it was so easy not to believe. After all, Guardiola was essentially a nobody back then; almost a legendary player, sure, but *only* a La Masia coach. That, especially at that time, didn't mean much to the general public, the fans and the press, all of whom would be quick to jump down his throat at the first sight of a struggle.

But while belief was scarce on the outside following a rough start to the season, it was still bubbling on the inside with major pieces of the jigsaw fully backing the coach. Laporta, even Johan Cruyff and Andrés Iniesta, were the ones reassuring the Catalan gaffer that he was doing the right thing – Laporta by sticking with his decision, Cruyff through his mentoring and columns for Catalan paper *El Periodico* at the time, and Iniesta, despite being this shy and introverted person, through a strong voice in the dressing room. That particular moment was described perfectly in the latter player's autobiography *The Artist*: 'Don't worry boss, we'll win it all. We're on the right path. Carry on like this, okay,' said Iniesta to his coach. 'We're in f***ing great shape, we're playing brilliantly. This year we're going to steamroll them all.'

And steamroll them they did. Barça soon went on a 20-match unbeaten streak, winning 19 and drawing a solitary one to take control of LaLiga. The Champions League was a whole different beast but one that was tamed in style and with dominance, nonetheless. Pep's machine would churn out goals and, on their way, conquer everything, including a treble of LaLiga, the Champions League and the Copa del Rey, becoming the first LaLiga club in history to do so in the same season.

Needless to say, Pep's first campaign as a Barcelona coach was more than just successful – it was dreamy. But the scary part is that as good as it was, the best was still yet to come. And, of course, their best had to include the most impressive version of Messi yet as well.

Intriguingly, though, Leo wasn't a happy camper when Pep first took over the team. The Argentine wanted to represent his national team at the Olympics in Beijing, but Laporta had other ideas, even fighting the Argentine Football Association on the matter. Ultimately, with some help from the Court of Arbitration for Sport, the decision was taken for Messi to stay with Barcelona and feature in their Champions League qualifier against Wisła Kraków. Needless to say, that played on Leo's mind a lot, casting doubts and affecting his overall happiness. Luckily, Guardiola, having previously won Olympic gold himself at the Barcelona Olympics in 1992, knew this moment could easily make or break a player and even affect his entire career.

Messi told TyC Sports in Argentina, explaining what had happened back then:

> Everyone said that it was so special and different and it really was a beautiful experience. Guardiola was phenomenal with me. No one wanted me to go; he was the one that gave me permission after a [pre-season] friendly against Fiorentina. He said to me: 'You want to go don't you? Well, you've got my permission. The only condition is that a member of our staff goes with you to look after you.'

That's how Guardiola managed to not only inspire a young Messi but also ensure he was committed and trusting of the process at hand.

This would turn out to be key when Pep asked Messi to once again change his role. Only this time it wouldn't take Leo out of his comfort zone but rather aim to bring the very best out of him. By 2011, Messi had already established himself as one of the best players in the world but the change to the iconic false 9 system and role would alter his, and Pep's, career drastically. As with everything else regarding the genius of Guardiola, this transformation would come about after careful studying of both his players' traits and the opposition. In May 2009, the two were ready to showcase it to the world in that famous 6-2 victory over Real Madrid in the heart of the capital.

'And that was an incredibly transformative move, not just by Pep, for that Barcelona team and for Messi, but for football. I think that was one of the great tactical moments of the 21st century,' Andy West told me during our chat on Leo's evolution. He's not wrong. Even though Messi was hardly the first player to enjoy the freedom of the false 9, that was still the moment that altered how football would be played in the years to come. Teams didn't know how to defend against it but would learn over time, adapting to the mechanisms Pep instilled in his Barcelona side.

Of course, it would take them time to get used to it, but slowly this Barça would force others to take note, not just of Messi but of general concepts the whole system brought into play. It would really be doing a disservice to the whole squad if all we talked about was Messi, but one of Pep's greatest challenges was to cater the squad and the tactics to the needs of the greatest player to have ever lived. He may have been just one of many amazing cogs that made that well-oiled machine the titan that it was but he was also undoubtedly the most important. Without him, the whole system wouldn't have made sense. Would it still have worked? Probably, but not as efficiently and cleanly as it did with him in the team. The same can be said for many others too, such as Iniesta or Xavi for example, but Messi was at the very core of that project.

To highlight how big an impact Pep had on him, we can once again consult the numbers. Messi played 219 matches for Barcelona while Guardiola was at the helm and managed to register 211 goals in that four-year period. This is also the time when we started to see the other side of his player profile: the creative playmaker that was still deep within but getting ready to burst out. With 97 assists to his name, Leo would drop not-so-subtle hints that another big change was just around the corner. When everything is said and done, this amounts to 308 goal contributions in just 219 matches he played for Pep defending the *Blaugrana* colours. The absolute peak of his powers would be seen in the now-legendary 2011/12 season when he racked up 73 goals across 60 matches. That tally rises to the record-breaking 91 when counting all goals for club and country for the calendar year 2012.

Despite Barcelona not being able to sustain the rampaging form of 2008/09 and the brilliance of 2010/11, Messi would still collect four Ballon d'Or trophies in the span of just four years, becoming the first player in the history of the sport to rack up so many in succession. At the beginning of Guardiola's reign, Leo was considered one of the best around, but by the time that story came to its natural conclusion, he was already in the discussion for the best player of all time.

Fast forward to 2022, with his seven Ballon d'Or and a plethora of other accomplishments despite Barcelona's struggles, that's still the case. Following Rijkaard's fall from grace, the team was in need of a new hope. And with Guardiola, they were given exactly that but also so much more. Messi, personally, profited immensely from Pep's appointment, as did most of the team – apart from those he immediately got rid of, of course, despite their stardom. But for Leo this was crucial because it moulded not just who he was at that time but also who he would become long after Pep was gone.

Álex Delmás outlines it perfectly: 'Without a doubt, Guardiola was the best coach Messi has ever had. After Pep, Messi started to understand the positional game much better.' This was key because Messi would indeed outlast Guardiola at Barcelona, so it was crucial that he understood the main principles, both for him personally and for the team as a collective. After all, he would be the one to carry the club forward through so many dark and happy times alike.

But what do we even know about his player profile in those golden years, and what were some of the main traits of Lionel Messi, who was about to mature into the best player in the world? At the same time, what tactics did Guardiola deploy to get the best out of the little magician? We'll aim to answer those specific questions and dive deep into Messi the player and the golden generation of Barcelona that won it all.

The False 9

Even though it may not be as complete as the versions that followed it, the false 9 era represents the absolute peak of Messi's abilities, both physically and technically. The key, of course, lies in the new-found freedom that Pep Guardiola's tactics afforded him and the role that unlocked his profile to flourish and ultimately ascend to new heights. This was also not an immediate change, as we've seen in the team analysis as well, since Leo would still be deployed as a winger in the first couple of seasons of Pep's tenure despite the new false 9 role being introduced as early as 2009. The epiphany happened leading up to the legendary *El Clásico* clash that saw Messi terrorise *Los Blancos* and lead Barcelona towards victory. For a youngster to do something like that against one of the biggest clubs in the world in one of the biggest matches on the planet is almost unheard of and will likely not be replicated any time soon either.

Jordi Costa outlines how the transition from winger to false 9 was indeed gradual, and it wasn't really until Pep's third season at the Camp Nou that the rebirth and reinvention of Messi would come to be:

> In Guardiola's first year, he [Messi] played the same way [as a wide winger], and in the second year, he

played as a winger or sometimes behind [Zlatan] Ibrahimović, but the real change happened in Guardiola's third year when he started to play as a 'false' centre-forward, close to Xavi and Iniesta and with very wide wingers (Pedro and Villa) opening spaces and offering deep lines of passing. To me, it was the best version of Messi.

And indeed, considering how menacing and free-flowing he was, calling that version of Messi the best one is very much warranted. But let's get back to the freedom Pep gave Leo, considering his movement and gravity.

Gravity is crucial here too; all players have it, but in bigger or smaller doses. To put it bluntly, gravity in football represents how big of a 'magnet' certain players are for defenders. Does their presence immediately put markers on alert? Does it pull them away from their positions? Does it break defensive structure? In Messi's case, it's a resounding yes to all three questions, so we can conclude that his gravity is an effective tool in the attacking phase. Looking at his heatmaps between 2009/10 and 2012/13, we can see that gradual transformation we talked about taking place.

In 2009/10, Messi was still very much a right-winger but with a tendency to cut inside on to his stronger left foot. Of course, seeing how his left is the deadlier one, this doesn't exactly come as a big surprise. Even in his youth, as we've seen in the previous chapters, when he was a more natural wide winger Messi would still aim to position himself to make the best use of his left foot. But as the years went by, this became more and more evident. While the early Guardiola years represent a mix between a natural and an inverted winger, the third season onward is where the real change would happen, as Costa explained previously.

LIONEL MESSI'S PASS RECEPTION
SECOND ERA

2009/10

DIRECTION OF PLAY

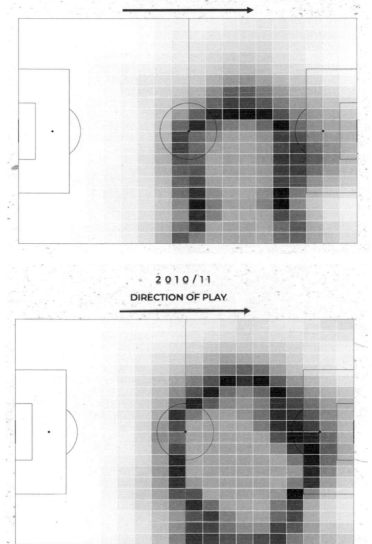

2010/11

DIRECTION OF PLAY

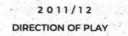

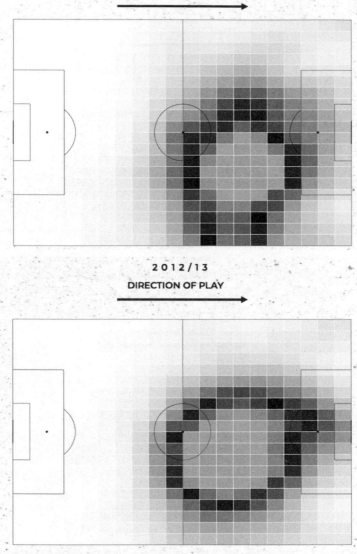

Notice how the heatmaps are slowly receding from the wide areas until he's fully focused on the central channels, starting in 2011/12 and culminating in 2012/13. These were also the years of Leo's explosion in front of goal, as we'll shortly see through the data as well. But what we have to remember is that, despite his godly lethality, back then Messi wasn't the complete forward we know today. Guardiola's arrival was the first step on Leo's journey to eventually becoming an elite playmaker too, which would only start to become apparent after Pep's departure and with Luis Enrique's appointment some years later.

The second era, Messi was more concerned with scoring goals than he was with setting them up. And, at first, that seemed more or less in line with what we've seen from him so far in his career. After all, not many electric and incredibly attack-minded dribblers normally evolve into complete forwards in the span of a couple of years. But then again, nothing about Messi is or ever was considered 'normal' in the footballing sense.

So looking at his chance creation and assists clusters next, the first huge difference that's most evident compared to the season prior is the sheer quantitative output. Under Rijkaard, Messi wasn't meant to be the creator nor did anyone think he would eventually grow into one. Under Pep, this was still largely true but subtle hints were starting to drop here and there.

Looking at the numbers, we can see a huge jump in output. Messi went from 158 chances created and 26 assists from 2005/06 to 2008/09 to 258 chances created and 54 assists from 2009/10 to 2012/13. The change and improvement are drastic to say the least, which could be said of almost all major aspects of his player profile during the jump from era one to era two. This is where most of his 'maturing' as a player would take place too. Costa, again, emphasises that exact point as well. 'When he was deployed in the "false" centre-forward position, he was a more mature player – he had more top players around

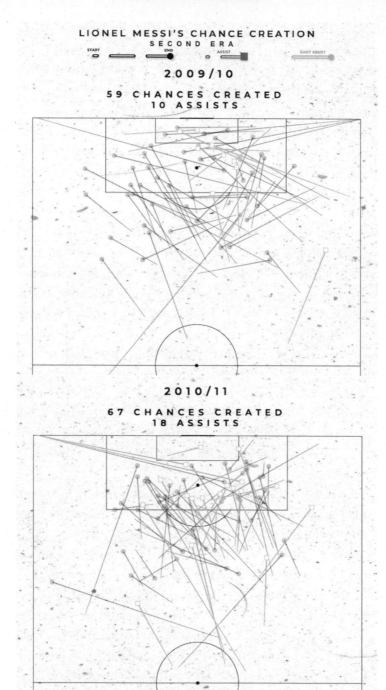

LIONEL MESSI'S CHANCE CREATION
SECOND ERA

START · END · ASSIST · SHOT ASSIST

2009/10

59 CHANCES CREATED
10 ASSISTS

2010/11

67 CHANCES CREATED
18 ASSISTS

2011/12

85 CHANCES CREATED
16 ASSISTS

2012/13

47 CHANCES CREATED
10 ASSISTS

him to make his life easier and, above all, he was closer to goal so his statistics increased automatically.' Compared to the first era, Leo would also start deploying passes from deeper and more central positions. This is highly beneficial because the centre, in general, is an area of greater strategic advantage in the attacking phase.

Just by being in the centre, Messi was closer to goal but also had easier access to both flanks, which was beneficial for someone whose passing range and vision were rapidly improving. It was the team as a collective that would prosper from that immensely in the years to come. It has to be noted, however, that Barcelona were arguably never as powerful as they were in Guardiola's years, and when the team as a whole is on such a high level, it inevitably balloons the individuals' output as well.

Of course, Messi was so good that it seemed he was playing an entirely different sport at times, but his feats wouldn't have been possible without such an extraordinary 'supporting' cast. Here, however, we'll focus more on Leo himself while turning the limelight to the rest of the ensemble in the team analysis chapter. So going back to Messi, next we'll take a look at his progressive carries in the opposition half.

The biggest difference compared to the first era is the starting position of all of the carries. As opposed to his early winger years, Messi was now much more centrally focused and would *almost* never hug the touchline and start his runs from the wide areas. Instead, he would receive possession in a deeper central position with a licence to progress in either direction afterwards. But this diversification of movement wouldn't really come to light until later on in his career, with the birth of the MSN partnership (Lionel Messi – Luis Suárez – Neymar Jr.).

Under Pep and in his false 9 years, Messi would largely advance towards the left and into 'zone 14', located in

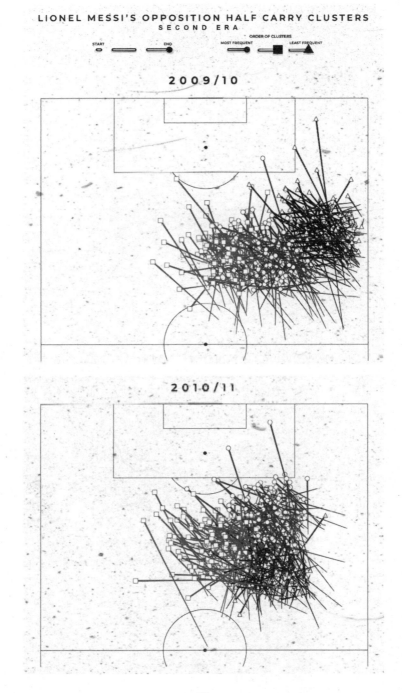

LIONEL MESSI'S OPPOSITION HALF CARRY CLUSTERS
SECOND ERA

ORDER OF CLUSTERS

START   END   MOST FREQUENT   LEAST FREQUENT

2009/10

2010/11

2011/12

2012/13

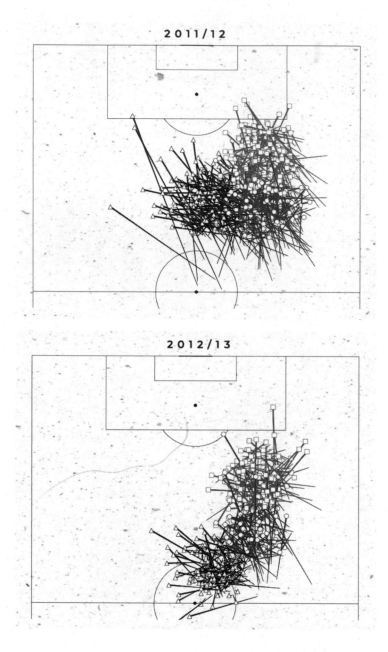

the central channel of the pitch, immediately outside the opposition's penalty area (see Appendix for a pitch grid). In 2012/13, we begin to see him dropping significantly deeper too, which was just a taste of what was to come very soon with Lucho (Enrique) and especially following the collapse of MSN. But as much as it's fun and interesting to dissect this aspect of his player profile, the false 9 Messi was never really about passing and creation. It left crumbs that would eventually lead to incredible revelations, sure, but at that point in Leo's career, his mind was firmly set on scoring and then scoring even more. Pep knew that. After all, this change in role and position was with the sole purpose of unleashing the beast from within. But before looking at shots and goals, let's first explore his penalty area entries first. There's quite a story to be told here too.

LIONEL MESSI'S OPEN PLAY PENALTY BOX ENTRIES
SECOND ERA

START ■——————→ END

2009/10

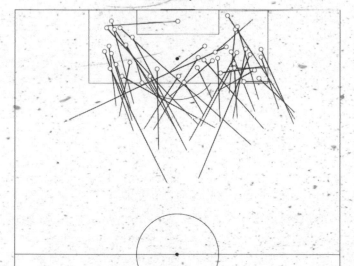

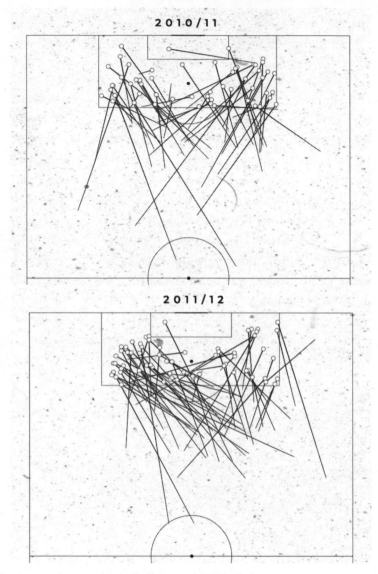

The first glaring difference is obviously the output itself. In his first seasons under Rijkaard, Messi was a very talented but still timid young winger who wouldn't attack the box nearly as much. This trait was about to change – and drastically so. But apart from just accessing the box much more often, Leo

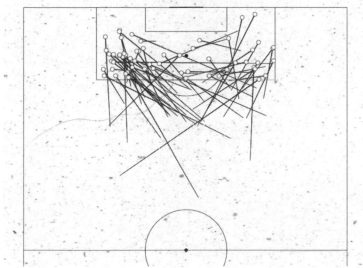

would also attack it from different angles. Being a natural right-winger in his youth, the only real access he had to the opposition's penalty area was through that right wing, largely resulting in entrances to the left of 'zone 18' and the right of 'zone 17' (area close to the right edge of the box). But with a far more central role, he would now suddenly get access to both sides of the box.

Naturally, that resulted in much more diverse penalty area entries than before, going towards both the left side and the right side of the box. But the real magic happened once he finally reached his favourite shooting positions. Marsden describes it perfectly: 'Here you've got the years where he moved to a more central position, where he was more difficult to pin down – the false 9. He's still got those original attributes where he's tricky and quick but becomes a goalscoring machine, a brutal finisher as well.'

And a goalscoring machine is very much the right way to describe Messi's false 9 days. He started shooting and

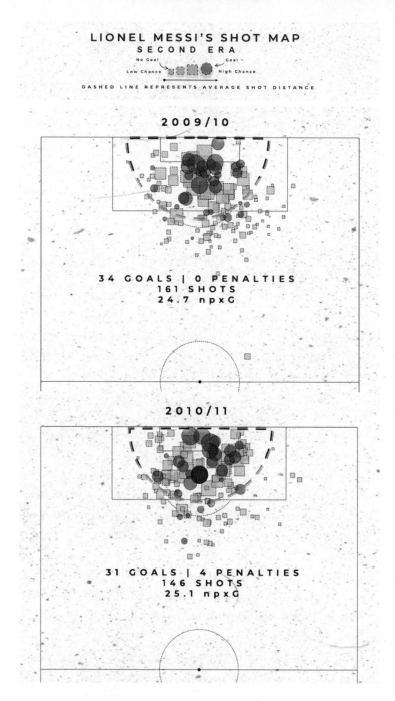

LIONEL MESSI'S SHOT MAP
SECOND ERA

No Goal — Goal
Low Chance — High Chance

DASHED LINE REPRESENTS AVERAGE SHOT DISTANCE

2009/10

34 GOALS | 0 PENALTIES
161 SHOTS
24.7 npxG

2010/11

31 GOALS | 4 PENALTIES
146 SHOTS
25.1 npxG

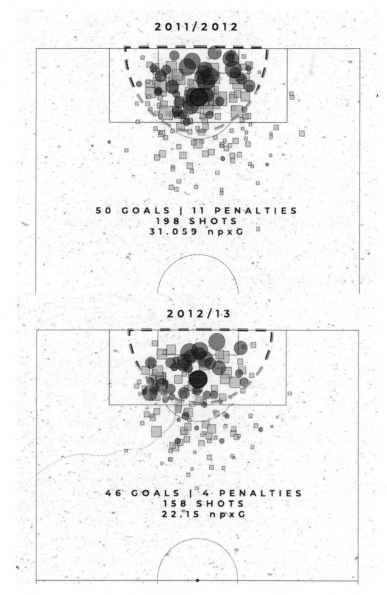

2011/2012

50 GOALS | 11 PENALTIES
198 SHOTS
31.059 npxG

2012/13

46 GOALS | 4 PENALTIES
158 SHOTS
22.15 npxG

scoring at an alarmingly high rate compared to seasons past, registering 161 goals from 663 shots and a total of 103.009 npxG. Needless to say, the 53 goals from the first era don't even come close to his prime false 9 years, nor do his 281 shots and the 36.789 npxG value. This Messi was a completely new and improved player compared to his old self, not only because of his lethal finishing, but also his general awareness and decision-making too.

Marsden explains it well again. 'Then there was a click when he realised: "Hang on, I can still do this and fit into the Barça style a bit more by knowing when to pass and when to run." So I guess awareness and decision-making was the first big improvement in his career.' This would come in handy for him personally, but it served the collective much more. Let's go back to the drawing board and see some of his most prominent traits in action.

The drawing board

So we've spoken at length about how this Messi was a natural goalscoring machine; a player who was finally in a role that sought to bring the very best out of him and allow him to stay closer to goal. In other words, the false 9 system aimed to ensure everything was set up perfectly for him to score as many goals as humanly possible. And score them he did – a lot. In this section of the book, we'll mainly look at two distinct features that best describe the Messi of this era: movement and lethality.

Of course, one could argue that both of those aspects have stayed with Leo throughout his whole career and it would very much be true. However, they were never as prevalent as in his false 9 years; the era of prime Lionel Messi. Different players peak at different times, and the same is true for players in different positions of the pitch, perhaps even different nationalities to a certain extent and, of course, different body types as well. So arguing that Messi was at his personal best somewhere around that record-breaking year of 2011 is difficult. After all, he kept getting better even when his goalscoring output went somewhat downhill. A lot of it was due to Barcelona's collective struggles as well. But going back to Messi and his false 9 traits, we'll now explore four different scenarios that best demonstrate the aforementioned aspects of movement and lethality.

Undoubtedly the best place to start is the very beginning, as ever. Guardiola introduced the false 9 Messi to the world in one of the biggest matches on the planet – *El Clásico* of May 2009. Interestingly, Barcelona opened the match in a more traditional 4-3-3 structure with Samuel Eto'o down the middle and Thierry Henry and Messi manning the flanks. However, at a certain point in the match, Eto'o and Messi swapped places, positioning the Argentine down the middle in a role that would shake the world of football to the core. Leo himself explains it best, speaking to LaLiga on DAZN:

> I remember that it was a surprise for me because I was called up the day before the game, was made to go to Guardiola's office at the Ciutat Esportiva, and I was told that he had been watching Madrid's games a lot, as he did with every opponent. He had been talking with Tito Vilanova and they had thought about me playing as a false 9. He was going to put Samuel and Thierry Henry on the outside, and I was going to play as the false centre-forward.

And that's exactly what happened, as we'll see in the following image. Both Messi and Henry are far deeper here while Eto'o pins the other defenders to the right. But the key is to track the movement of Real Madrid's defenders too – Fabio Cannavaro started man-marking Messi even as the Argentine dropped far deeper than usual for a centre-forward. Of course, Leo wasn't a traditional centre-forward at that point, but no one apart from Barcelona's camp was in on that *little* secret.

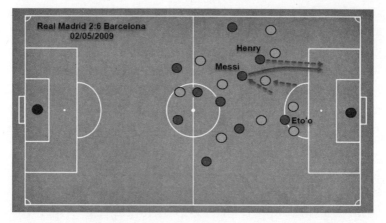

This meant that Henry was isolated against Sergio Ramos in a one vs one duel and with dynamic superiority on his side. Since forwards are facing the direction of play and defenders usually have their backs towards their own goal – or at the very best are positioned at an angle towards it – they can accelerate much more quickly and burn them in a foot race. That's exactly what happened to Ramos as he tried to stop the marauding Frenchman. All Messi had to do was chip the ball over Cannavaro and into Henry's path. Of course, that's not to say that it was a simple pass to deploy, and certainly not the type he would soon become capable of playing. This example is perfect because it demonstrates that even without scoring the goal himself, Messi's movement and gravity were enough to drastically influence the opposition's backline and ultimately the result.

After all, Henry was able to exploit the space behind Real Madrid's defence solely because Messi had previously dragged the Italian centre-back out of his position. And that's exactly what this type of movement does – it creates space, either for Messi personally or for his team-mates.

'The idea was that Madrid's centre-backs would follow me out, and the two fast wingers that we had would go around the back. In fact, one of Henry's goals was like that. It was a surprise for us and for Madrid,' Messi told DAZN, perfectly describing what had happened at the Santiago Bernabéu Stadium that night in 2009.

But let's explore another example with a very similar outcome, more than two years after the famous 6-2 against Real Madrid. This time we're looking at a match against Villarreal in August 2011, when Barcelona won 5-0. You'll notice most of the results in our examples are devastating *Azulgrana* wins, as this was a more common occurrence at that time.

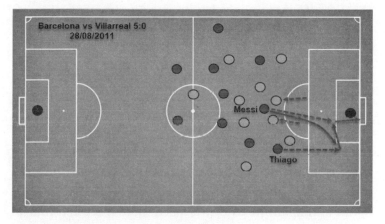

In this instance, it's Messi's movement that once again creates the space and enables a wide isolation for his team-mate. Instead of Henry, we have Thiago playing the main role. As soon as the Villarreal defenders come out to mark Leo, the Spanish midfielder is gifted a one vs one duel, which he crucially wins, and soon after he can collect the ball following another brilliant pass from La Pulga.

You'll notice how Messi's passing is gradually improving at this point already. As was mentioned previously as well, at this time in his career Leo wasn't exactly famous for his playmaking abilities, but the world would start to pick up small hints that this would eventually be the case in the not-so-distant future. Interestingly, however, as much as this sequence is all about creating space and threading a lovely pass, it's also about how Messi's positioning is giving him an advantage too. Yes, Thiago gets an isolated duel out wide but, at the same time, two of Villarreal's defenders are now out of position.

Messi was never exactly the fastest footballer on the planet but his acceleration and turn of pace were always elite, even in his older days. And back in 2011 he was quite pacy as well. For that reason, it's quite easy for him to quickly go from standing still and deploying the pass to his team-mate to sprinting past the defenders and into the box for a return pass from Thiago. And that's exactly what happens as he gets possession back in front of the goalkeeper and steers it home.

These runs into the box would soon become a trademark of his, especially in the years to come, as this tendency to attack the box from deep would become more and more prevalent in his player profile. But in the false 9 era, Messi also perfected the technique of delayed runs as well. He would still attack the box, but while the defenders continued their runs back to the penalty area, he would slow down and let them settle before asking for the ball with much more space and time to do his magic. This is another very important aspect we have to discuss. At that time, teams weren't sure how to properly defend against these tactics, as we'll see in the team analysis part as well, and that meant that sometimes they would make the wrong decision of leaving Messi alone and unmarked between the lines – big mistake. For a great example, we'll consult the sequence against Viktoria Plzeň in November 2011.

Here, Messi is once again deep but, despite that, the opposition is very late to react, initially refusing to break their structure to immediately press him. It's also here that we come back to the original decisional crisis the false 9 role presents to opponents: Do I press and leave space behind my back? Or do I stand my ground but then risk leaving the player unmarked? Plzeň's players opt for the latter option and it's not until Leo receives possession that they decide to go for a collapse on the ball. At that point, however, it was already far too late.

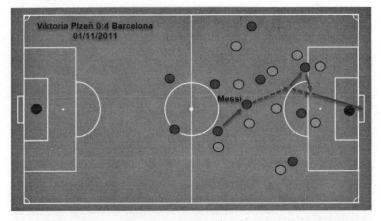

The Argentine can receive the ball cleanly, and as soon as he does, he starts one of his trademark marauding runs down the middle of the pitch. Upon closing in on the box, he plays a quick one-two with one of his team-mates and then fires a thunderbolt past the opposition goalkeeper. You'll quickly notice this is something he would do far more regularly in the years to come, sometimes after beating multiple defenders on his own. But in the false 9 years of the Guardiola era, he often didn't have to beat them at all because he was gifted far too much space and time on the ball in the first place. Of course, nowadays, he's almost never afforded such luxury anymore as teams have learned from others' mistakes. But that was hardly the case back then and our final example will help us demonstrate it once more.

This time, we'll visit Barcelona's 4-0 victory over Osasuna in January 2012. This sequence is fairly similar to the previous one against Villarreal as Messi is once again afforded far too much space and time. Xavi Hernández finds him with a ball that effortlessly breaks the lines and Leo receives possession in one of his favourite positions just outside the opposition box. From there – especially for all of us reading this at least a decade after this beauty of a goal – ensues a fairly common sequence.

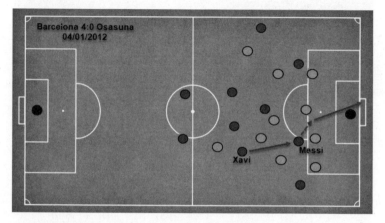

I've decided to include this example precisely because it would become a trademark Lionel Messi goal for years to come. Shortly after receiving the ball, he cuts in ever so slightly, positions himself on his stronger left foot and lets loose just around the edge of the penalty area for a perfect finish straight into the left corner – absolutely no chance for the goalkeeper. Not back then in 2012 and not ten years later, even when they all know what's coming. That *was* and still *is* the beauty of Messi's goals – you know perfectly well what he's going to do, and yet there's so little you can do to stop him.

But the real test for both Leo and Pep in those years was taking Messi's unparalleled talent and seamlessly incorporating it within the squad. Fortunately for the Catalan giants, that's exactly what happened.

Pep's Barça

When Pep Guardiola was handed the reins of FC Barcelona back in 2008/09, the club wasn't in as dire a state as when Rijkaard was taking over from Van Gaal and Antić years before. However, following two barren seasons in the Dutchman's final stretch, the Catalans were once more in need of a complete overhaul, both tactically and mentally. So that's exactly what Pep did – he changed *everything*.

Graham Hunter told me:

> It wasn't just about Pep and Messi, it was about making the team better. When Pep came in, everything changed – the press, the positional play, the spaces which could be created for Messi, people's timekeeping, rest times and how often they travelled to games.
>
> Everything changed and Messi wasn't someone who didn't get affected by things around him. He's a genius who's had the benefit of playing in utterly exceptional teams. It's not just the best version of Messi but of every player in that era.

And just as it was the case at the beginning of Rijkaard's era, a change in personnel was needed to give the team a boost. Only this time it was more about protecting the club's clear assets from bad influences within the team. Even though they were among the biggest names on the sheet, Ronaldinho and Deco were the ones whose personalities and behaviour the new coach wouldn't tolerate for long. Both stars departed the club that season and made way for new signings, such as Dani Alves,

Aleksandr Hleb, Seydou Keita and the promotion of Sergio Busquets from Barcelona B.

However, it's important to understand that this wasn't necessarily an entirely sporting decision. Had their behaviour been better, perhaps Pep could have found a way to incorporate them into the team. A talent like Ronaldinho, despite his eventual and rapid decline, would have surely found a place in the jigsaw that was being assembled by the Catalan gaffer. Of course, that would potentially change the whole outlook of the squad and inevitably affect Messi's development too. After all, Ronaldinho was the star until Pep's arrival and it's difficult to imagine Leo in such a free role with the Brazilian by his side. Ronaldinho's sacrifice, therefore, alongside the likes of Deco, was necessary and for the greater good but also for Messi's own good.

Since the Argentine was very fond of the two and considered them close friends, their bad influence was a risk the club and Pep weren't ready to take, as Hunter explains:

> The reason Guardiola got rid of those two [Ronaldinho and Deco, wasn't because it was impossible to play good football. It was predominantly because they were setting an example for Messi, which was a bad one. If you talk about the best version of Leo under Pep, it was first of all because of a change of lifestyle but second of all because two very big friends who would become big temptations were kicked out of the club. And that helped!

In 2008/09, Barcelona would win everything while playing beautiful attacking football. But even though they were already being heralded as one of the best teams football had ever seen, *the best* was yet to come. By 2011, Pep would somehow not only match the intensity, commitment and quality of his former team but also perfect it. If the 2009 team managed to surprise the world, the 2011 one would completely dominate and ultimately conquer it.

It was also during those years that Barcelona popularised the principles of positional play, aiming to dominate matches by achieving superiorities across the pitch, either through numerical, qualitative, positional or dynamic advantages. And as I've already alluded to earlier, it was all about the collective with Pep, not about an individual star player. As big and as influential as someone like Messi was for the team, the rest of the squad was also carefully picked. They needed to have profiles capable of bringing Guardiola's vision to life, and while it required some tweaking along the way, Pep managed to build the machine he longed for in the end.

Víctor Valdés retained his position between the sticks but would also see his role completely change. The thought of a ball-playing goalkeeper was a distant one at that time, and even though Valdés was an amazing keeper in his own right, he had no idea what was coming next. 'That's when I thought this guy [Guardiola] was nuts. He told me that I was the one who was going to start every play by passing the ball to them [the centre-backs],' Valdés explained in *The Guardian*'s movie *Take the Ball, Pass the Ball*. Luckily, ahead of him were always players of great quality on the ball. In 2008/09, Pep brought Gerard Piqué back to the club and in 2010/11 Javier Mascherano would join too. Soon, the two would create an excellent tandem in the backline, with Carles Puyol, who had a diminished role due to injuries by then, still in the rotation when he was fit and ready to feature.

Together, the three players in the first phase of Barcelona's build-up were the crucial pieces in making the machine tick well. Perhaps the most important additions, however, would

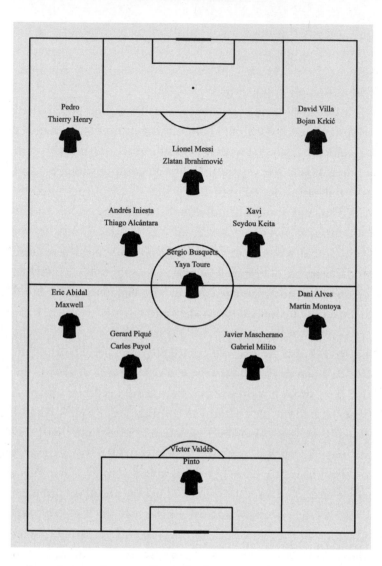

end up being the transfers of Alves to replace Oleguer and Belletti at right-back, and David Villa a couple of years later. Together with the emerging Pedro, the ex-Valencia star would form industrious wide options that would enable Messi to have the freedom he needed to dominate and terrorise every defence out there.

Pep's formations varied over the years, but generally he stuck with the traditional 4-3-3 most of the time. However, as he himself would often say, formations are nothing more than just numbers on a piece of paper and ultimately hold little value in the grand scheme of things. This proved to be true in theory and in practice too as his players were used in a plethora of different positions and roles depending on the opposition, their structure, movement and tendencies on and off the ball.

Of course, it's impossible to talk about roles and not mention Pep's brainchild – the false 9, as Andy West explained to me:

> He [Pep] thought about taking this player [Messi] and maximising his strengths, and maybe minimising his weaknesses, and building the team around him. And the conclusion was to put him in the centre of the field, get him closer to goal and to Xavi and Iniesta. It took years before anyone had a handle on how to deal with him in that role.

He's right. Guardiola's system was very much used to get the best out of Leo, but also to get the best out of every single player in the squad too. Barcelona's structure from as early as 2008 all the way through to 2011 and 2012 aimed to maximise every team member's potential to create a collective that's infinitely stronger than the sum of its parts. Of course, the fact it had some outrageously good parts helped a tad too. But working and playing as one helped a lot. Just as it was important under Rijkaard, coordinated movement and awareness played a key role in Barcelona's tactics under Pep. Everyone had to know the basic principles of positional play and how to implement them in any given situation. In other words, every player had a well-defined role they had to know in their sleep.

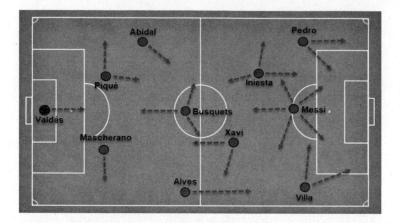

The structure that you see in the image closely resembles Barcelona's traditional 4-3-3 system, but in possession that could quickly change to variations of 3-4-3 or a 3-3-4. The centre-backs, as mentioned earlier, were key to ball progression, advancing play through sharp vertical passes and always staying wide and pushing up when necessary. That's why it was crucial that they were comfortable in possession even when under intense pressure. Their movement opened the space for Busquets to drop into. This pivot role between the centre-backs would soon become synonymous with the La Masia midfielder and he would end up deploying it for more than a decade into the future. Of course, other players such as Keita or Yaya Touré would occasionally stake a claim for Busquets's spot, but would ultimately fade in comparison to what 'Busi' could bring to the table. His footballing knowledge, awareness and passing ability ensured Barcelona always had a way out in any given scenario and against high-pressing teams too.

Xavi and Iniesta were the other two pieces of the midfield trident, different but equally as important. The former was still more of a controller, adjusting the tempo that was being set by Busquets from a deeper role. Xavi was positioned to the right but would step closer to the backline if the team

needed more personnel to breach the defensive block or just
escape the press. Iniesta, on the other hand, was free to
join the attack, akin to what Deco would often do under
Rijkaard too. However, Iniesta's combination of dribbling,
speed and vision made him an incredibly potent outlet down
the left that would occasionally slot in on the wings too, such
was his quality. Together, the three magicians would form
the greatest Barcelona midfield trident to date and one that
will be difficult, if not impossible, to eclipse. Xavi, Iniesta
and Busquets were undoubtedly the hub of the whole team.
Without them, everything would have likely fallen apart.

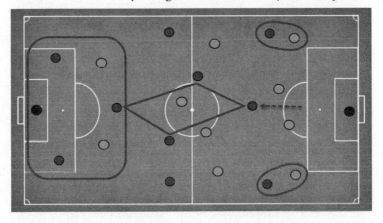

This graphic shows us the basic principles in Guardiola's build-
up stage. Numerical superiority in the first phase of play was
crucial, so the goalkeeper and the centre-backs were often
joined by the dropping pivot. Of course, this varied depending
on the defensive structure of the opposition. If the other team
pressed with two, Barcelona would only need three players to
overload them. If more were committed to the press, Barcelona
would answer accordingly. Essentially, it was a simple premise
that required courage in possession. Having your centre-backs
and goalkeeper dictate play and direct the attack from the back
was a risky approach but also one that yielded a lot if executed

well. Playing out from the back pulled the opposition forward, stretching their lines and creating space between them. This superiority would continue higher up the pitch too as Messi would drop to combine with the midfield. Together, their technical quality would overpower most, if not all, teams, and Barcelona often didn't need numerical superiority when their qualitative dominance was so overwhelming. Just matching the opposition in numbers was enough to outplay them. The same was true with the wingers. Having them isolated against their markers was huge as they had the quality to beat the defenders and get into favourable positions.

With that in mind, the real firepower was unsurprisingly up front. Before we touch upon Leo in that 4-3-3 false 9 role, we have to discuss the wingers a bit more. Villa and Pedro were players of exceptional individual quality but their roles were quite industrious within Pep's system. The former was the more central presence that would cut inside and exploit space behind the opposition's line. At times, he would even act as the second striker in tandem with Messi himself. Pedro, on the other hand, was more of a traditional winger, albeit not entirely so. He would stretch the pitch and provide width, sure, but was also very intelligent, timing his runs well and dragging markers to create space.

And then there's Messi. 'It was complete, unrestrained freedom but with responsibility. There was just nothing he couldn't do at that point,' Andy West told me back when we were chatting about Leo for *Legacy Magazine*. Freedom really is the key word here. Pep had completely overhauled Leo's role, but with that change and added responsibility came the perks of freedom. Messi was now the star of the team, not Ronaldinho, so he could let loose and let his creative juices flow. Ultimately, that was Pep's idea – his tactics would get the team to the final third and ensure the stage was set and ready for them. But the final step was only theirs to take and they would be tasked with making the magic happen through their own quality, both as incredible individuals but also as an unstoppable collective.

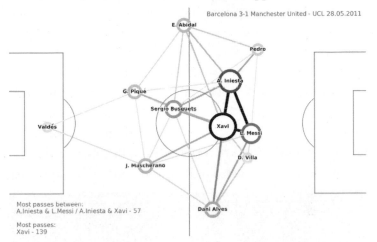

Barcelona 3-1 Manchester United - UCL 28.05.2011

Most passes between:
A.Iniesta & L.Messi / A.Iniesta & Xavi - 57

Most passes:
Xavi - 139

This graphic shows the pass map from Barcelona's now-legendary match against Manchester United in the Champions League Final. Interestingly, it shows us almost all the traits of Guardiola's structure perfectly. You can see the high positioning of the centre-backs and their vertical passing and connection with the midfield. The recycling and retaining power of Barcelona's core was on an incredible level as all the players had the technical quality and awareness to keep the ball and dismantle the opposition. Finding gaps in the opposition's structure was crucial but Pep achieved it by ensuring superiorities on the pitch. It doesn't take long to highlight the most important pieces of the puzzle down that middle channel of the pitch.

The size of the circles represents the number of passes and, unsurprisingly, all three of Xavi, Iniesta and Messi have the biggest influence on the team. We can also add Busquets into that mix but it was mostly about the trio slightly higher up the pitch.

Another very important thing to note here is the positioning of all of them. Messi is very close to both Xavi and Iniesta so the three could always combine in tight spaces and outplay the opposition by both outnumbering them and also through the sheer level of their technical quality being so much higher than everyone else's. And to Messi, having someone of such quality close to him was paramount.

'In Iniesta's book, Messi talked about when things were difficult, he wanted Iniesta as close to him as possible. Someone else he could trust to keep and move the ball,' Sid Lowe remembers. Pep knew this too and that getting the best out of Messi was by surrounding him with such players. By

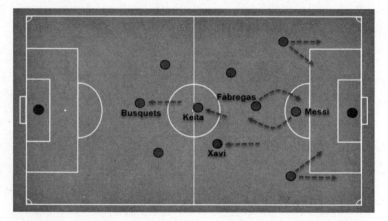

ensuring that, he would also ensure the build-up phase and overall control of the game was tilted in Barcelona's favour right from the get-go. Still, the means of actually getting them to the final third would vary almost on a match-to-match basis.

I've mentioned before how Pep's structures were fluid but still revolved around two main systems: the 4-3-3 we've seen earlier in this chapter, and the more attacking 3-diamond-3 that would often be deployed against teams who predominantly sat in a deep block.

And here, it's very important to mention the likes of Cesc Fàbregas, Alexis Sánchez, Seydou Keita or even Thiago Alcântara. Of course, we know those players weren't always a part of Pep's strongest Barcelona but they still played a role in some of its variations, this one in particular. Guardiola loved their flexibility, as playing Keita deeper alongside Xavi meant that Busquets could drop between the centre-backs. Fàbregas, on the other hand, formed an excellent partnership with Messi and the two would swap places to maximise Leo's effectiveness and Barcelona's unpredictability. Cesc had great attacking instinct, while also being capable of supporting the build-up next to the midfielders, giving Messi more freedom to roam the final third. But since the Argentine himself still had the tendency to drop deeper, it meant Fàbregas could take his place higher up the pitch.

Another change this system brought to Barcelona is how they used their wide players, namely full-backs and wingers. The classic 4-3-3 with Pedro and Villa often had the former staying wide and the latter cutting in centrally but, in this diamond structure, Pep prioritised natural wingers since the full-backs were essentially sacrificed for a three-at-the-back system. The roles of wide wingers were left for the likes of Sánchez, Pedro or even Iniesta and Fàbregas at times, as Guardiola continued tinkering with the squad. Of course, as I've mentioned before, the goal was to get his talented group to the final third and then let them do their thing. As a general rule of thumb, the final third tactics depended largely on the opposition and would change week in, week out. However, there were still some set aspects the team would adhere to.

If we go back to the original 4-3-3 with a false 9 Messi, we can discern some major concepts while still taking into consideration the freedom that was given to the players. Messi played a huge role because he was the crown jewel of that team, regardless of how important the rest of the squad was. And, needless to say, they were incredibly important. Still, Leo's movement was key to creating overloads and enabling progression down both flanks of the pitch. Of course, he preferred to move towards the right side where he would often combine with the likes of Xavi and Alves. The midfielder, in particular, had a knack of finding the Argentine in the right half-space or just ahead of the opposition box. It's from there that we would then see Messi turn quickly, beat a marker or two and unleash a curled shot into the far corner, rattling the inside of the net.

But Messi didn't even have to touch the ball to be extremely effective at dismantling the opposition, something which is true to this very day too. Due to the immense gravity he possesses, even the tiniest of movements would put opposing teams on high alert, making them readjust accordingly. With Leo being as lethal and as important to mark as he was, him dropping deep would inevitably create chaos in the opposition's backline. And as soon as the pieces start moving, space appears elsewhere.

This is where players like Xavi, Iniesta or even Busquets come into play. Their vision and awareness were simply on a different level, allowing Barcelona to fully exploit Messi's space creation, both on and off the ball. If Messi created space through dribbling and then passing the ball to one of the midfielders, they had no issue finding other players who were now unmarked due to Leo's actions. On the other hand, if Messi created space through off-the-ball movement, the midfielders would again deploy killer passes to find other priority targets. In short, Messi was the crucial piece of the jigsaw, but it was the collective that shone the most because of it.

As Álex Delmás told me when we talked about Leo in Pep's Barcelona for *Legacy Magazine*:

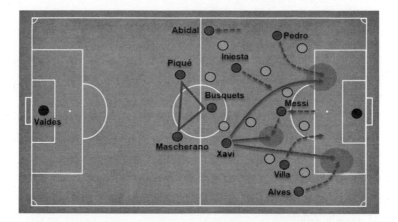

He [Messi] was the difference. It was a great team, a magnificent team and it was a team that even without Messi would also have fought for all the titles. But he was the next step; he was the one to push the team past their limits. That was maybe the best moment in the best player in history's career.

His understanding of the team's needs, and the team's understanding of his needs were the key to success. Pep knew that unleashing Messi would take Barcelona to new heights, but the creation of that false 9 Leo was never with such an individualistic goal in mind. For Guardiola, the team came first. Yes, he adored Messi, and even years after leaving the club he would still talk about how that team was all about the little Argentine wizard. There's no escaping the absolutely crucial role he played, but Pep's greatest achievement was creating a team that complemented Messi's vast, godly repertoire so smoothly as opposed to completely succumbing to it.

'Barcelona had clear ideas of how to attack and defend as a collective but also with enough freedom for the individual talent like Messi, Xavi or Iniesta,' explains Álex Delmás. And understanding that is key to understanding why the Catalans would crumble in the future. Their tactics, philosophy and main principles were no longer suited to playing well as a collective and that was their undoing. The birth of the false 9 in that fabled 6-2 against Real Madrid is also a by-product of Pep trying his very best to find the easiest and most efficient way to hurt Barcelona's eternal rivals.

Graham Hunter told me the coach spent a long time tinkering, trying to understand the opposition better and, ultimately, he found gaps that could best be exploited with Messi playing centrally. So yes, in a way, it was a change that would unlock Leo's best version of himself but at that time it was made with the team's collective superiority in mind. Hunter explained:

> The decision tree [behind the false 9] was studying Real Madrid, looking at the vast space between the midfield and the central defenders – who were a bit slow in those days – and figuring out how to exploit it. Then he decided, 'I'll put Messi there, and with his brain and with his speed, we'll exploit the space.

That was the true reason for the creation of the false 9. There were gaps in the opposition's structure that only Leo could fully exploit. But even though being an inverted winger would often take him centrally, it wasn't enough; the team would best benefit from his swapping places with Samuel Eto'o, so Pep did just that. And the rest, as they say, is history.

Of course, when talking about the power of the collective, it's impossible not to discuss the defensive phase of play. Barcelona are well known for their incredibly creative attacking sequences but, as the modern-day version of the team can attest to, it doesn't matter much if you don't have a good defence.

Interestingly, despite largely revolutionary approaches to defending that we saw from Pep's team, the basic premise remained the same. Guardiola probably explained it best when he talked about his Manchester City team not exactly being full of defensive juggernauts, but rather their stability in possession that enabled them to have excellent out-of-possession phases too:

> Patience doesn't mean lazy, slow. It's the ball. If you have the ball, you are in order and everything is stable. Stability is the ball. It's not about defending 40 metres behind or 40 metres up front, or high pressing, or defending, or long balls, or whatever. To be stable as a team, it's the ball, no more than that.

This isn't something Pep has come up with just now. It's his whole philosophy. As odd as it may sound, his Barcelona perfected what we call 'defending with the ball'. The basic premise behind that admittedly strange term is having a very stable in-possession structure that lends itself nicely to a good defensive transition but, more importantly, one that ensures the ball can be retained at all times. For that to happen, Barcelona had to have inch-perfect space occupation, complementary movement and incredible awareness, both of their team-mates' and the opposition's positioning. 'Death by a thousand passes', as it was famously called. This is also where the derogatory term 'tiki-taka' comes from. Some confuse tiki-taka for a heavy positional and possession-based style of play, while the two couldn't be more different. The former suggests passing for the sake of passing. The latter, however, is a strong premise and emphasis on ensuring superiorities are always held across all thirds of the pitch, all with the aim of outplaying the opposition.

But even teams as capable on the ball as Pep's Manchester City and Barcelona lose possession, which is where the stable on-the-ball structure comes into play again. By ensuring optimal spacing and compactness in his teams, especially that legendary Barcelona squad, Guardiola managed to perfect the popular 'six-second rule'. According to him, his players were instructed to press aggressively in an attempt to immediately recover the ball within the first six seconds of losing possession. If they failed to regain it within that time span, they would then drop back into their standard defensive structure.

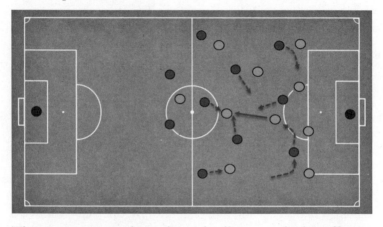

The very intense and coordinated collapse resulted in effective counter-pressing and would often end with the ball being regained in higher parts of the pitch as close to the opposition's goal as possible. Interestingly, even Messi would participate in such actions. As Graham Hunter told me, 'If Messi pressed, everyone pressed.' And that's probably the biggest proof of Pep's philosophy that he managed to instil. If you get the star player to work as hard as the rotational option from the bench, you know you've done your job well. Of course, Messi's defensive work rate and contribution would inevitably start to drop with each passing year, but at his – and Barcelona's – peak, he was as willing and as engaged in all phases of play. With everyone working as one and everyone around the peak of their powers, Barcelona were all-powerful and all-conquering.

The fairy tale, of course, wouldn't last forever, and soon Pep would leave Barcelona feeling drained and exhausted. The years immediately following his departure were, sadly, extremely tough, in both football and non-football matters surrounding the club. Tito Vilanova's stint was short but very exciting. Being Guardiola's understudy, Tito managed to preserve the philosophy and even add his personal twist to some of the tactics. His Barcelona were more flexible and more direct while retaining some of the fundamental aspects that were, and still are, at the club's core. Sadly, tragedy struck, leading to Tito losing his battle with cancer, and everyone suffered because of it. But, as ever, Messi would continue developing and shining, with another evolution around the corner. Just when we thought Leo wouldn't be able to further surprise us with more tricks, he comes up with something extraordinary once more. The world would soon meet the mythical MSN trident, and Messi ... well, he would never be the same again.

Chapter 4

Total Player

The Birth of MSN

The post-Pep Guardiola era was always going to be a rude awakening for Barcelona. It's one thing to eventually reach the peak, but somehow balancing on top of it for prolonged periods of time is sometimes an even more daunting task. The years immediately following Pep's departure were very difficult, both on and off the pitch. The team suffered a psychological blow after Tito Vilanova, the man chosen and destined to continue preaching Guardiola's teachings, was diagnosed with cancer, a fight he would sadly ultimately lose on 25 April 2014, aged 45. Needless to say, this shook not only the club and the players but also the footballing world to the core.

Suddenly, Barcelona found themselves without a clear direction once more and were in need of a breath of fresh air – again. Gerardo 'Tata' Martino was the one to take over the team halfway through 2013, but his tenure was as short as it was downright strange. By the end of the 2013/14 season the Argentine was gone, making way for a coach who would mark the third grand era of Barcelona's rich history: Luis 'Lucho' Enrique Martínez. But while the successful seasons between 2014 and 2017 were largely the new coach's own doing, they were also marked by perhaps the most feared attacking trio in the history of the club, and arguably the sport: Messi, Suárez and Neymar formed the infamous MSN partnership.

What started with Luis Suárez's €82.3m move to Barcelona from Liverpool in the summer of 2014 ended in an incredible 364 goals between the magical trio in 450 matches. Together, Lionel Messi, Suárez and Neymar Júnior created a beast that would devour opposition through their sheer power of will, but also through ingenuity that was born through their connection that stretched far further than the edges of the pitch. 'The friendship that we had was something very beautiful. What I miss from Barcelona and about Barcelona is these two, due to the joy we had on a daily basis,' insisted Neymar even after his record and heartbreaking move to PSG at the end of their incredible story.

This is perhaps even as important as the skill all three possessed individually. There's no denying that in their prime years MSN were remarkable as individual players, but when you put those parts together – combining Messi's godly ability, Neymar's chaos and Suárez's lethality – you get an unstoppable trio with seemingly limitless potential. The end result?: 450 matches, 364 goals, 173 assists and seven trophies – two LaLiga titles, three Copa del Rey crowns, a Champions League medal and a Club World Cup on the side. The 2014/15 season was undeniably the most successful one for Barcelona as a collective as they managed to clinch the treble, the second one in the club's history.

The years that followed were less successful but still impressive, culminating in an overdrawn drama that saw Neymar swap the *blaugrana* of Barcelona for the blue and red of Paris, a team he had helped destroy in the historic *Remontada* at the Camp Nou not long before. That was the poetic end of an era that marked heights the Catalans haven't reached, let alone eclipsed, ever since. The modern-day Barcelona are still a team in transition and very much fighting to rediscover the identity that has been lost.

Intriguingly, however, as we'll see in the coming chapters, Lucho's Barcelona wasn't something the purists in Catalonia would easily approve of either. Having the most feared and lethal attacking trident in the club's and perhaps the sport's history and not completely surrendering to its influence is almost impossible. Barcelona would, of course, suffer from this over-reliance on superstar influence for years to come, even after the complete disintegration of the MSN partnership. But despite their unearthly highs, the trio also needed time to fully click. Even with Suárez's transfer being done and dusted in the summer of 2014, the Uruguayan and the fans would have to wait four months, until his ban for biting Giorgio Chiellini during the 2014 World Cup was lifted, for him to be able to share the pitch with his soon-to-be best friends in Messi and Neymar.

The long-awaited day, however, was soon forgotten as the mystic MSN faltered to a rampaging Real Madrid in a 3-1 *El Clásico* defeat, showing glimpses of things to come but also a lack of understanding and any kind of connection on the pitch. That, of course, was understandable considering they had never played together before, but the sheer talent and potential they had between them were already palpable at that early stage. After all, on his debut and in a match of such magnitude, Suárez managed to assist Neymar for the opening goal and the Brazilian's first-ever *Clásico* strike. A storm was brewing, and soon it would be unleashed all over Spain and Europe.

However, it would take them some time to properly gel together, and with Lucho's near-constant rotations of the team in the early stages of the 2014/15 campaign, not many would have predicted such a glorious end to the season. Needless to say, MSN played a huge part in that too. But, as ever, Messi was and would continue to be the core piece of the jigsaw. Ironically, that was perhaps one of the reasons for Neymar's departure.

'Neymar and Messi? I wouldn't put two captains on the same ship,' said the late, legendary Johan Cruyff when asked about the power duo. But that's exactly what Barcelona were at that time. One ship. Two captains. It was never going to be sustainable, and in an attempt to leave Messi's shadow, the Brazilian had to leave not just the club but the league as a whole, sealing his €222m transfer to the 'City of Light'. That, together with the whole MSN era, had a huge impact on the player Leo was and would eventually become. Prior to the arrival of his partners in crime, he was the only real superstar of the team despite the squad featuring giants of the footballing industry. During Guardiola's reign, the world was starting to differentiate between the super-talented player Messi always was, and the best player of all time he would soon be viewed as by most. It was quite sensational that the latter version of the Argentine wizard would willingly take a back seat so others could thrive.

'With Neymar and Suárez, he was a very generous player and sort of played different roles depending on what he thought the team needed and depending on whether Neymar and Suárez were there or not. Sometimes he even willingly took a back seat,' explained Samuel Marsden during our chat about Leo. This plays a key role in Messi's player development too, something we'll explore in more detail in the chapters to come. Barcelona had this giant of a player and suddenly they added two more into the mix and hoped for the best. The Real Madrid *Galácticos* of the early 2000s or the Barcelona variant of the late 2010s tell a very cautionary tale of why such things rarely work out for the best. In the Catalans' case, however, it not only worked out – at least for a while – but ended up writing one of the most successful eras in the club's history.

Maybe era is the wrong word here, though. After all, the team with MSN enjoyed one absurdly impactful season before slowly but surely faltering in the years to come, until eventually Neymar broke the band up. For Messi personally, however, these were very challenging years. Not only did he suddenly have to adapt to having Neymar and Suárez around and gelling with them properly, but his failures with the national team pushed him to his limits, eventually forcing the Argentine to announce an early retirement from servitude to his country. This, of course, was a decision he would soon revoke, but at the time it moulded his persona, both in his own eyes and the eyes of the public.

Messi as a player is very demanding, which is something coaches with less authority in the years to come would soon find out, but in the MSN era he was far happier simply because he was surrounded by players he would also consider close friends of his. Even after both Neymar and Suárez were long gone, the friendship would remain. Messi himself confirmed this when speaking to *Goal* about Suárez:

> I didn't like the way he left. I didn't think he deserved to leave like that. He went for free to a team that is fighting for the same things as us. I speak to Luis almost every day, and between the three of us, we have a very good relationship.

This confirms two things about Messi: firstly, his friendship with the other two parts of the MSN partnership, and secondly, how important that friendship is for him personally. The psychological part shouldn't be ignored here.

Let's not forget that despite having Suárez and Neymar by his side, Messi was still by far the most influential of the three, scoring 153 goals in the time the three of them spent playing together. That's 32 more than Suárez's 121 and 63 more than Neymar's 90. Barcelona as a collective ended up winning almost everything in those three seasons, but Messi individually claimed another Ballon d'Or in 2015 and the European Golden Shoe at the end of the 2016/17 season too. Individually, and despite the added stardom in the team, he was still excelling.

But to excel, Messi had to evolve once more, altering his playing style and preferences to accommodate the other two superhumans that were now playing alongside him. One might ask why it worked with Neymar and Suárez and not with, say, Griezmann and Coutinho; in football, and with Messi especially, it's all about the right profiles. Not everyone fits every system and not every player profile is compatible with any other profile. Messi, for instance, needs runners, verticality and pace around him. Perhaps even more than that he needs highly technical players to combine with. During the MSN era, he had those things and he had a coach who could embrace the trio's insatiable hunger for goals and properly weaponise it.

Leo accepted that, for the MSN partnership to work, he had to become a right-winger once more. Not in the traditional sense, of course, but the false 9 position was now replaced with a natural striker in Suárez, while the left flank had a natural winger in Neymar. Over time, the Brazilian would evolve past that role too, but in that period at Barcelona, he was a very different player to the one he is now. That suited Lucho's tactics just fine and his main goal was, to put it bluntly, to make his star front three tick along smoothly. The fact that the three of them contributed to a staggering 80 per cent of all Barcelona goals in their period together is astonishing, to say the least.

If we look exclusively at LaLiga, the combined numbers are just as unreal: 250 goals from 299 matches, amounting to a goal every 102 minutes. With an attack like that, everything else was secondary. That, unfortunately, is true in both a tactical and personnel sense, as many players were relegated to inferior roles just to keep the trident happy and provided for. But how exactly did Luis Enrique's Barcelona play, and what was Messi's role in that monstrous squad?

We've already mentioned he had to adapt once more for MSN to prosper, but what sort of changes did he go through in that period stretching from Suárez's arrival and all the way to Neymar's departure? We'll look at it in more detail, starting with Leo's profile under Lucho.

The Playmaker

Perhaps the most impressive of all aspects of Messi's player development is the sheer ability to adapt and overcome obstacles. Nowadays, not many players stay at the same club for so long, and not many would have it in them to not only survive the constant changes but also thrive on them. Messi is one of those players. Following the incredibly successful era under Guardiola where his role had perhaps changed the most, few could have predicted what came next.

Leo would drift back towards the right wing to accommodate Suárez and Neymar's inclusion in the jigsaw, but there was much more to that tweak than initially met the eye. If Pep's Messi was the ultimate goalscoring threat, the version that soon followed would completely eclipse his former self, allowing his player profile to flourish into a 'Messi that could do it all', as Álex Delmás so neatly put it. Since there were other players in the team who could rack up the goals in his absence or instead of him, Leo would still present a great threat to the opposition, only now it would start to come in two different ways: through goals, which was a constant in his player profile by now, but also through assists and chance creation, which was then a novelty in his kit.

Freedom still played a huge role in the whole story. Pep was the first one to give Messi so much freedom of movement, and this was when things finally started to click. While this was perhaps most evident in that false 9 era, at least until the post-MSN period, it somehow became an ever-present aspect of his role. Why? Well, coaches discovered that Messi worked best when given that permission to roam free and express himself beyond the constraints of highly limiting structures. Of course, that doesn't mean he wouldn't follow the main principles of Barcelona's positional play, but he was given a lot more trust to do what he thought was best in almost any given situation.

Jordi Costa emphasises this freedom of movement too: 'When Luis Suárez arrived at Barcelona, Messi returned to the right wing, but now with all the freedom to drift inside.' This sort of freedom can be seen in his heatmap too, which we'll dissect next in the diagrams.

With the arrival of Suárez and Neymar, we see Messi's positioning once again shift towards the flanks. On paper, he was a winger again, but this time – compared to the first era when he was a natural winger – he would act more like an inverted one, starting wide but inevitably drifting inwards when in possession. But the intriguing part is how the heatmaps not only change from era to era, but also from season to season. While the 2013/14 and 2016/17 campaigns saw him far more centrally focused, the two in between – 2014/15 and 2015/16 – were a mix of wide and central positioning.

This shows he's adaptable to his team's and team-mates' needs, but also that he's far more difficult to successfully defend against. In the years prior, Messi would wreak havoc in isolated duels out wide, then by putting defenders in a decisional crisis

LIONEL MESSI'S PASS RECEPTION
THIRD ERA

2013/14
DIRECTION OF PLAY

2014/15
DIRECTION OF PLAY

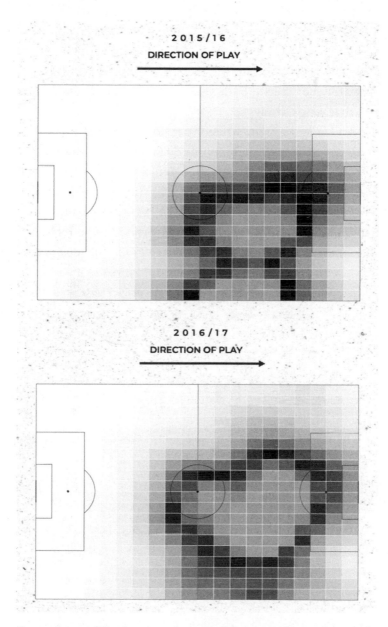

2015/16

DIRECTION OF PLAY

2016/17

DIRECTION OF PLAY

down the middle, but now he was able to combine what made him unpredictable in the first era with what made him lethal in the second to become the complete package, as analyst Albert

Blaya explains, 'Starting from the wing, he is able to dominate inside, outside, far and near ... He became the total player.' Nowadays, we associate Messi with a complete forward – a forward who's able to both score and create at an elite level – but that wasn't always so.

And, interestingly, while Guardiola managed to awaken the true goalscorer in him, it was during the third era that his profile started to become more complete, as his passing also improved. While that wouldn't necessarily be visible in pure assists (52 from 2013/14 to 2016/17 vs 54 from 2009/10 to 2012/13), it certainly was in chances created as he registered 306 in the third era compared to 'only' 258 in the second one.

LIONEL MESSI'S CHANCE CREATION
THIRD ERA
START   END   ASSIST   SHOT ASSIST

2013/14
71 CHANCES CREATED
11 ASSISTS

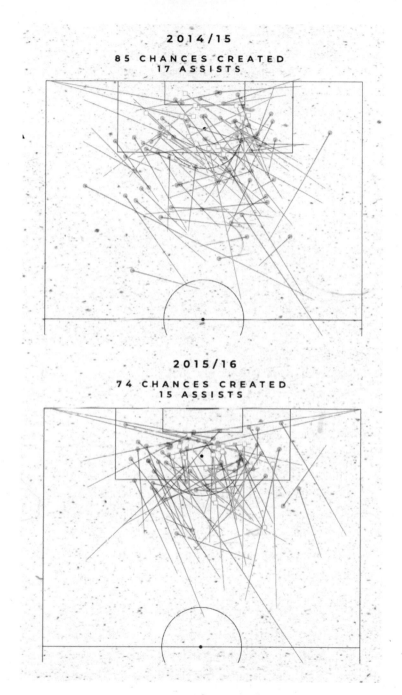

2014/15

85 CHANCES CREATED
17 ASSISTS

2015/16

74 CHANCES CREATED
15 ASSISTS

This new side of Messi caught many by surprise, including experts such as Michael Cox, who says there weren't many signs in the Argentine's early years that would hint towards him becoming such an elite playmaker:

> Of course he's still been an amazing, prolific dribbler, but when he broke through I didn't see too many signs he'd become the best through-ball player in the world. To me, that has added something important and means he's been able to play for the team, not just for himself.

This last part of Cox's quote is as important if not even more so than the first part. To be 'able to play for the team, not just for himself' is something that we take for granted in the present day, simply because it seems like a very common part of his kit. But the younger versions of Messi were far more individualistic, as we've seen in the previous chapters of this book. In the MSN era, Leo started working for the team much more, understanding when to take a back seat while still being a highly influential figure within the squad, and also simply realising he *can* take a back seat if needed. Sadly, in the years that followed, those opportunities would become scarce as the team continued on a very heavy downward spiral after the highs of the Luis Enrique era.

But staying with the MSN incarnation of Messi, this is also when the gradual decline towards the deeper areas began too. Pep's idea with the false 9 was to bring Leo closer to goal, but as the years went by, it seemed like the Argentine was slowly drifting away from it while still retaining his godly goalscoring proficiency. This can be seen in the chances/assists graph, from earlier, and also in the carries that we'll dissect next.

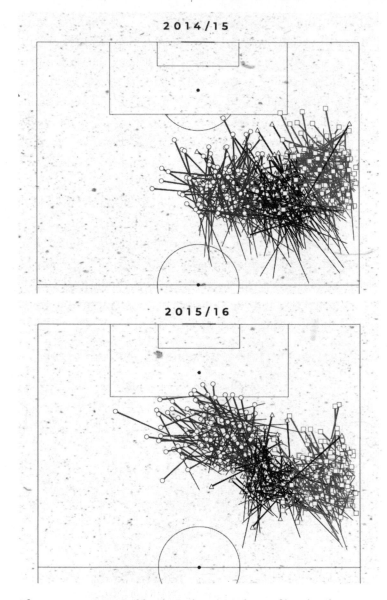

If you cast your mind back to the second era of his development, you'll remember Messi was slowly dropping deeper and deeper in the carries graphs too. This trend then continued into the third era, albeit on a slightly smaller scale. What's prevalent

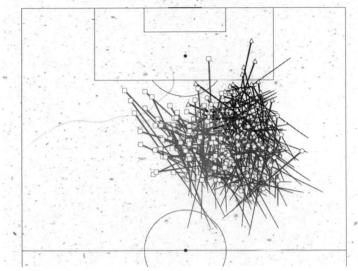

here, however, is the starting point of those carries. With the introduction of the MSN trident, Leo was once again deployed as a right-winger, only this time with the tendency to cut inside, resulting in his carries starting wide on the right but ending more centrally and towards the left side of the pitch.

However, in line with the adaptability of his profile we discussed earlier in this chapter, Messi would now dribble to both the outside and the inside, depending on the needs of the team. If Dani Alves was on the overlap, Leo would gladly drift inside with the ball before potentially combining with the Brazilian to the right. But if the overlap wasn't on, Messi could still dribble towards the outside and keep the width himself while someone such as Suárez attacked space through the middle. Naturally, with his approach altered once more, the way in which he attacked the box was different too, albeit not necessarily dramatically so in every aspect.

Two of the major changes in Messi's approach have to do with distance to goal and the direction of his box penetration.

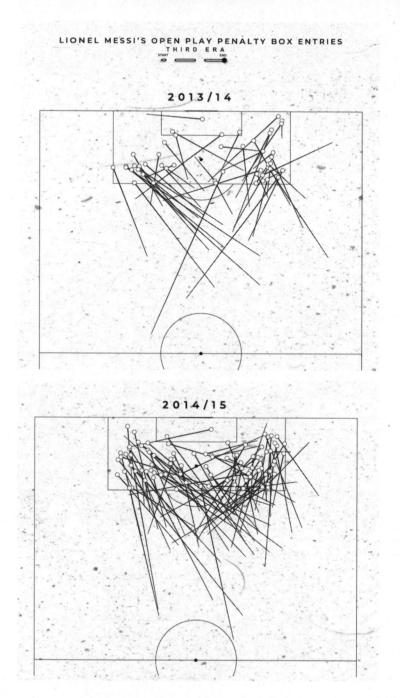

LIONEL MESSI'S OPEN PLAY PENALTY BOX ENTRIES
THIRD ERA

START   END

2013/14

2014/15

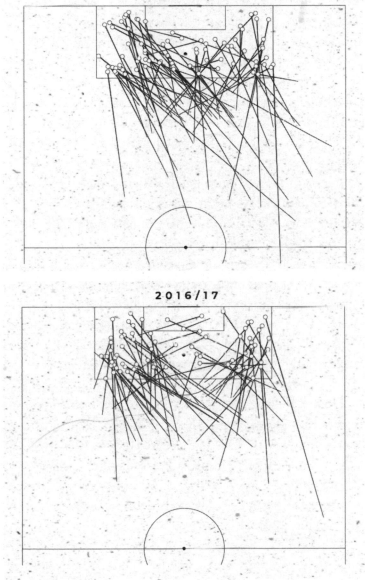

The common theme that follows his player development throughout this book is his tendency to keep dropping deeper and deeper. We've already established that this process started even at the end of the second era, but wouldn't be as noticeable until the beginning of the third one. A similar pattern can be seen with his penalty area entries, which seem to have a somewhat deeper starting location too. But even more importantly, instead of almost exclusively attacking the opposition's box from right to left, Messi would now diversify his approach and enter the penalty area drifting towards both flanks.

Again, this is very much in line with the unpredictable and complete nature of his profile that was starting to be moulded in those years under Luis Enrique and post-Pep Guardiola.

One further thing that we need to mention about his penalty area entries is the sheer quantity. Even with the likes of Suárez and Neymar in the team, Messi's hunger for goals was still on the rise. But this increase in output is also closely related to the heavy verticality that Lucho's Barcelona demonstrated. They were far more direct, fast and decisive with him than in the years prior, which also played a part in slightly tweaking Messi's approach too.

Finally, we have to address arguably the most important aspect of his player profile: shooting and goalscoring ability. Interestingly, with 134 goals scored from 2013/14 until 2016/17, the overall output decreased, partly because of the unearthly figures of 2011/12 and 2012/13, which alone amounted to 96 out of the total of 161 goals scored from 2009/10 until 2012/13.

But despite scoring fewer goals, Leo was starting to shoot much more and from far greater distances too, a trend that would continue in the years to come. In the third era, he would take 683 shots, 20 more than in the previous four seasons,

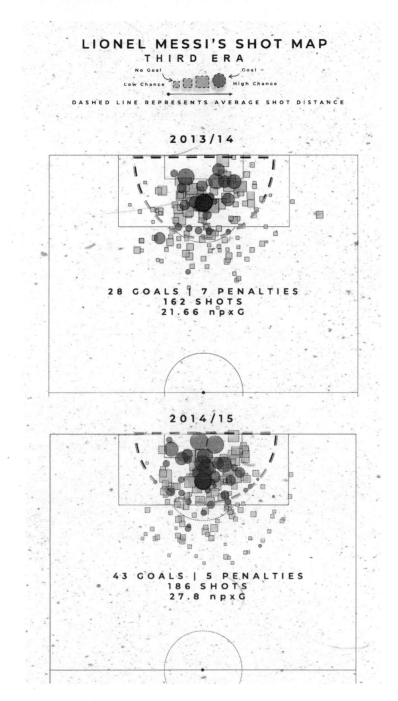

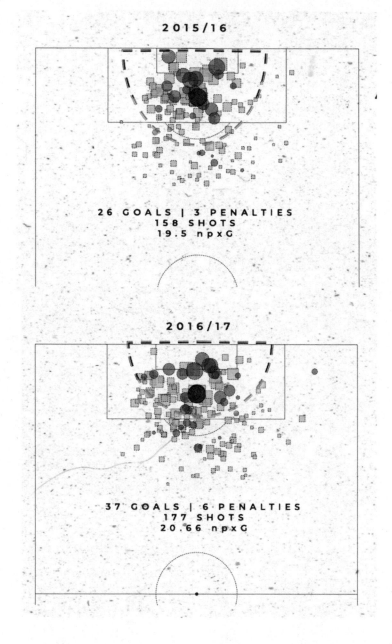

2015/16

26 GOALS | 3 PENALTIES
158 SHOTS
19.5 npxG

2016/17

37 GOALS | 6 PENALTIES
177 SHOTS
20.66 npxG

accumulating 89.62 npxG in the process, also significantly lower than the 103.009 he registered in the previous era.

Of course, all of this was connected to the big change in role and profile he was going through. After all, having been turned into a lethal finisher, Messi was now developing the other side of his attacking spectrum, focusing on creating as much as scoring himself. And as his positioning continued to drop deeper and deeper, that affected his shooting, dribbling and carries altogether.

But despite a statistical decline in output, the Argentine would still be a terror to opposing defences and a key cog in Lucho's machine that would soon take over Spain, with Europe following closely. Let's jump to the tactical boards to see these changes in action.

The drawing board

Luis Enrique's Barcelona were far more direct and vertical, as we'll see in the team analysis section a bit later. This inevitably impacted how Messi operated on the pitch. It has to be said, however, that MSN needed time to click and it took some positional changes to finally get them to gel properly. The main issue was, ironically, getting Messi and Suárez to complement each other. Initially, Leo was hesitant to let go of the false 9 role that had brought him so much success, which resulted in the Uruguayan being deployed out wide instead.

However, soon Lucho realised this wouldn't work, and while Messi was comfortable in his position, Suárez wasn't.

That's when the switch back to the winger role happened for Leo. But as we've repeatedly mentioned throughout this book and especially in this chapter, he wasn't the winger he had once been. 'This was the period where he was still unquestionably the best around, often playing from the right with Suárez up front,' recalled Michael Cox once more, reiterating how Messi continued his dominance, but this time from a slightly altered position. 'I don't think he's had too many problems adjusting to wherever he's been asked to play, to be honest, he usually finds a way to get the ball in his between-the-lines inside-right position.' We've seen from the data that Leo was now boasting a much broader arsenal while retaining his hunger for goals and a very direct and fast approach. This gelled well with how Enrique envisioned his Barcelona to operate too.

In the following graphics, we'll explore those traits in more detail and highlight some of Messi's most important connections on the pitch. Keep in mind that this is the beginning of the playmaker Messi, and in this era we would finally see his passing repertoire flourish into elite levels, taking the world by surprise. Other players we simply have to highlight here as well are, of course, Neymar and Suárez, but also Dani Alves, Barcelona's right-back at the time. There are more, but these three are key in understanding the player Messi was in that period. Let's start with the last player, as the other two's combinations and telepathic understanding is now a part of Barcelona's folklore.

When people think of Alves, they think attacking full-back. This may be true, but as we also saw in the chapters before, the Brazilian wouldn't necessarily attack the final third exclusively through his overlaps once Messi inevitably inverted towards the centre. The two were very creative and even diversified their approach on a match-to-match basis. Our first example explores Alves underlapping and Messi inverting too, which is a combination we've rarely seen at modern-day Barcelona.

Notice how Messi starts out wide once the ball reaches him and Alves is a pseudo-third centre-back/inverted right-back who pushes up through an underlap. The play starts

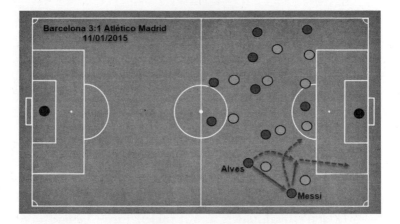

with the Brazilian in possession of the ball deep on the pitch and he quickly deploys a pass towards Leo before making a penetrating run towards the opposition's box. Messi receives the ball, essentially hugging the touchline, immediately sends it back to Alves and runs towards the centre and 'zone 14'. If you cast your mind back to his third-era shot maps earlier in this chapter, you'll notice that this is the area Messi absolutely loved to shoot from.

Ideally, Alves would be able to either whip in a cross or send a cut-back to the Argentine just outside or just inside the penalty area. From there, La Pulga is almost at his most dangerous and the opposition know it too. This particular sequence against Atlético Madrid doesn't result in a goal or a shot because Alves is tackled before a cut-back or a cross can be deployed, but it still shows us one of the possible approaches and interactions between the two. Interestingly, that match was largely regarded as the first great performance of the MSN partnership and one that started the avalanche that would soon cover the whole of Spain, and eventually Europe too.

Going back to the team's directness and Messi's tendency to attack the box, we'll now explore an example in which he's the one on the underlap, profiting from his team-mates' movement.

We've already explained how Leo thrives with certain profiles that can create space for him and no one personified that trait quite like Suárez himself. El Pistolero was the ideal partner in crime for the Argentine with Gabriele Marcotti perfectly summarising why for ESPN:

> Suárez's presence was critical in allowing Messi to return to the right wing on a more permanent basis, though always with a licence to come inside and create. Suárez was perhaps the perfect synthesis of [Zlatan] Ibrahimović and [Samuel] Eto'o; he had Ibrahimović's technical ability, but Eto'o's work rate and intelligent movement.

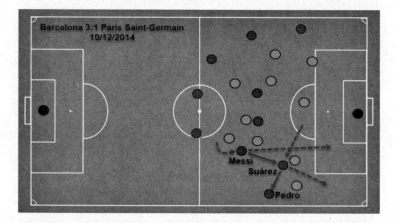

In the second graphic, we can see Messi's relationship with Suárez in one of Lucho's experimental 4-4-2 systems with the pair up front and Pedro and Neymar as wide midfielders just behind them. This meant the Argentine wouldn't necessarily start by hugging the touchline but could drop deeper and then penetrate the box with piercing runs through the right half-space. In the sequence against PSG, he receives the ball around the halfway line, beats his first marker and then combines with

Suárez, who drops deeper and drifts wide to pull David Luiz out of position. This opens the channel for Messi to advance, and with Pedro stretching the backline even more, Leo has lots of space to work with.

Suárez also continues the run towards the right flank, ensuring PSG's defenders can't collapse on Messi in the half-space. Unfortunately for Barcelona, this sequence doesn't see Messi receive the ball inside the box as the French team manage to plug their defensive holes before the Catalans can inflict more serious damage. But this action is intended to demonstrate how other players' movement and positioning aimed to give Messi the freedom he craves so much. Again, we come back to complementary profiles; the likes of Suárez and Pedro are certainly the right type of players whose work rate and tendencies go hand in hand with Leo's role. Interestingly, this was also the first match in which all three of Messi, Suárez and Neymar found themselves on the scoresheet, a sight that would almost become commonplace by the time they finished their glorious run.

Now we'll turn our gaze towards Neymar a bit more. His profile at that time was drastically different to the one we see nowadays. The Brazilian of the MSN era was far more electric, direct and more akin to a natural winger with pace and incredible one vs one prowess. This meant he had the ability to stretch the pitch and attack space, something that fit Lucho's tactics – and Messi's preferences – perfectly. But Neymar's importance was far from just tactical; it was also emotional. As Sid Lowe puts it:

> One of the reasons I always thought Neymar was brilliant – despite some of his flaws – was that he was one of those players that didn't necessarily say, 'I've got to give the ball to Messi, Messi is better than me.' He

didn't feel inferior to him, or not obviously inferior. The right thing about that is I don't think Messi felt that either. He liked the fact there was a player who didn't just say 'Messi will do it'.

In the years following the Brazilian's departure, apart from perhaps Suárez, the team would never have a player of that mould again. Sure, Suárez himself had great respect for Messi and would always admit how the Argentine was miles ahead of him, but he would still score plenty of goals and assert himself regardless. Neymar was similar. He wasn't at Leo's level but he had this arrogance and courage to take people on and push play forward without relying on Messi all the time. That doesn't mean the two weren't compatible, or that they didn't work together often; on the contrary, it made their relationship that much stronger, on and off the pitch. The next graphic explores the signature switch from right to left, from Messi to Neymar, which preceded the famous Messi–Alba connection that would soon be born too.

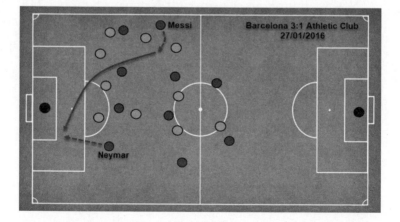

Once again, Messi starts this sequence against Athletic Club by hugging the touchline and receiving the ball directly from the backline. As soon as he's in possession of the ball, however, he cuts inside on his stronger left foot, and immediately after spotting Neymar's run on the opposite side, deploys a deadly – albeit slightly mishit – diagonal pass into the opposition's box. At that point in 2016, this switch had already become a formidable weapon for Barça and would continue to be for years to come. After Neymar's departure, Jordi Alba would fill the Brazilian's role with a rather similar effect. Instead of Neymar finishing those chances himself, the Spanish full-back would look to cut the ball back into Leo's path inside the box.

However, here we also have to highlight the completeness of Messi's profile. Before, we saw him as the ideal partner for Alves on the right, but now, suddenly, he was expanding his repertoire to accommodate for a similarly influential presence on the other side of the pitch with both Neymar and Alba. 'You have the fact that Messi was the best partner for Dani Alves on the right but then you also get the fact that he was the best partner for Jordi Alba on the left. There you can see the evolution of things that Messi does,' Sid Lowe explained to me.

The last example we'll explore in this chapter is from the now-legendary *Remontada* match against PSG in the

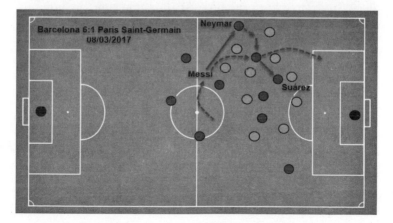

Champions League in March of 2017. The graphic shows us the MSN partnership in action, as well as demonstrating Messi's personal tendencies at the time quite well. The sequence starts with Leo very deep on the pitch and drifting from the right side to the left, as was and still is common for him.

Note that Messi's positioning starts where his name is in the graphic and ends inside the opposition box. The dot between Neymar and Suárez is his position at the moment of the link-up play between all three. After drifting towards the left, Leo deploys a pass towards Neymar, who's hugging the touchline and attracting markers.

The moment the ball leaves his foot, Messi starts the run towards the half-space where Neymar soon finds him after inverting ever so slightly. Suárez, in the meantime, also drops deeper, dragging his marker and then receiving the ball with his back to goal.

Ideally, the Uruguayan would be able to either turn or immediately lay it off to Messi, who's attacking the box. Sadly, after twisting and turning a bit, Suárez eventually loses possession and the attack breaks up. Still, the sequence demonstrates how Leo was slowly starting to drop deep but still aggressively attacking the box. At the same time, it shows us that Barcelona's tendency to focus on the left side of the pitch was very much present, even before the modern-day iteration became famous for it. But the 6-1 comeback against PSG was very much MSN's swansong, and soon Neymar would pack his bags and leave for Paris.

And that, unfortunately, was the domino that fell and ultimately led to the Catalan giants' modern-day crisis, one piece at a time. But it would also push Messi into perhaps his most impressive form yet and the final stage – at least for now – of his player profile evolution.

Lucho's Barça

Taking Pep Guardiola's formula and improving on it was never going to be an easy task. His Barcelona revolutionised not only the way the *Azulgrana* played, but how football was perceived as a whole. Building on that legacy – or rather, deciding how to build on that legacy in the years following Pep's departure – was always going to define Barça's short- and long-term future. But Luis Enrique Martínez García, or 'Lucho', the coach to lead the next all-conquering generation from 2014 until 2017, would do it his own way. Lucho's Barça were still adhering to the club's core principles but they were also unique in how they approached the game. It was quite clear that replicating his predecessor's success and principles would be difficult with the change of guard already in progress with new and different profiles coming into the club.

Luis Enrique faced a plethora of different obstacles upon arriving at the Camp Nou, both on and off the pitch, partly because of Guardiola's shadow that was still looming strong above Catalonia. Tito Vilanova's sad passing robbed Barcelona of Pep's natural successor and 'Tata' Martino was unsuited to the job from the very beginning. So it was up to Lucho to restore the club's greatness once more; at Barcelona, however, it's never just about the silverware but also how you get there. Identity, style of play and philosophy are terms the Catalans hold dear but also terms that would, unfortunately, get lost in the years to come. Under Lucho, however, the basic principles of possession-based football and winning through domination were still present, albeit in slightly different but not necessarily worse forms.

Under the Spaniard's helm, Barcelona were a different animal; still dangerous and hungry to win, but less inclined to follow Pep's formula to achieve it. In the eyes of the public, many fans and media included, this wasn't a good sign. Just like Guardiola, Lucho is a man who likes to experiment and tinker with the squad until he finds the best possible solution. This process of trial and error, however, wasn't something the Barcelona faithful were so accustomed to. At the beginning of the new coach's stint, the Catalans didn't exactly have a stable system or a very clear starting XI as Lucho often rotated and tried players in different positions. After all, even the fabled MSN trio didn't click right from the start, which was due to Messi still wanting to be deployed down the middle, relegating Luis Suárez to the wide role to the right.

Needless to say, the Uruguayan's effectiveness as the team's winger was greatly reduced, and soon Lucho would have to make the difficult decision to scrap the legendary false 9 system that was introduced by Pep. Not to mention that by that time the rest of the footballing world had already adapted to Barcelona's approach, breaching the gap that was once so large. Of course, Messi would still remain very dominant in that role, but it wasn't as effective as it used to be in the years when Barcelona had first introduced the concept. Albert Blaya explained to me that the role would finally meet its limitations once Messi started getting more and more involved in all phases of play. We've seen from Leo's player profile in the previous chapters how his skill set was expanding into that of a total player during Luis Enrique's stint. However, since some key figures such as Xavi and Iniesta were getting older, and wingers such as Alexis Sánchez, Pedro and David Villa were either gone or soon to be sold, all the space Messi used to have between the lines was becoming increasingly smaller.

This was true for several different reasons. Firstly, Barcelona weren't as sharp anymore, but Leo was also no longer surrounded with profiles that were as complementary to his own. Opponents were also now more familiar with Barcelona's false 9 system that made Messi a prime target down the middle channels.

'Once his role asks him to participate and influence all heights and phases, that position [the false 9] falls short. This is because Barcelona were getting worse: Xavi was slower, the wingers less aggressive ... He [Messi] runs out of space in

which to play – he drowns!' Blaya explained when we spoke about Messi in his false 9 role in the post-Pep eras. And this is very true. Leo's individual quality is often enough to create space on its own, but wingers such as Pedro and Villa were key to the role's overwhelming success in the past. But now they were gone, sold or replaced, so the false 9 had lost its punch. Lucho had to find his own brainchild; and from that, MSN was born.

The revolution had started a season before Luis Enrique's arrival when Barcelona secured the services of a wunderkind by the name of Neymar Júnior for a reported fee of around £79.2m. A year later, Lucho himself would ask for more signings, gradually moulding the team in his image. So in came the likes of Ivan Rakitić, Marc-André ter Stegen, Claudio Bravo and the biggest of them all: Luis Suárez from Liverpool for around £73.5m. All of them would end up playing huge roles in the new coach's story but also continue to be prevalent figures even after his departure. All except Bravo, that is, who would eventually be completely displaced by the new German keeper.

Interestingly, most of the core signings all arrived in Lucho's first season, with the exception of perhaps Samuel Umtiti, a centre-back signing from Olympique Lyonnais in 2016/17, nearing the end of the Spaniard's tenure. Sadly, 2014/15 marked the last excellent season for transfers that Barcelona would have for a long time. But as we've already seen with the eras preceding this one, a good rebuild almost always includes incomings as well as outgoings. Lucho had to endure departures of club legends such as Carles Puyol and Víctor Valdés, as well as losing young talent such as Jonathan dos Santos to Villarreal and Bojan Krkić to Stoke City. That same season, Cesc Fàbregas and Alexis Sánchez were sold to Chelsea and Arsenal, respectively, and following the treble-winning season, Xavi Hernández packed his bags for Al-Sadd SC. It was quite clear that Luis Enrique's job wouldn't be an easy one.

But after a lot of experimentation, everything finally clicked and a brand-new Barcelona would emerge from the gutters. As previously alluded to, this Barcelona was the same, but different simultaneously. Throughout Lucho's tenure, we would still see them dominate matches and control the ball with conviction, averaging over 60 per cent possession from 2014/15 all the way through to 2016/17. But as opposed to being a very methodical and patient team like the one led by Guardiola, this Barcelona was far more aggressive, direct and packed a punch in transition too.

With that in mind, the roles of many players were overhauled once more with the exception of the backline. The centre-backs and the goalkeeper were still crucial in the first phase of build-up and acted as the main progressors for the team, but with Valdés gone, the club had to secure a keeper that would fit the profile just as well. In came both Bravo, the initial first choice Lucho used throughout the LaLiga campaign, and Ter Stegen, the soon-to-be undisputed starter who, at first, only featured in Champions League matches. Both players had quality on the ball and slotted well into the team. Ahead of them were some familiar faces in Gerard Piqué, Javier Mascherano and Dani Alves, with the addition of Jordi Alba on the left side from the 2012/13 season.

As is the case with almost every iteration of Barcelona in their modern history, this quintet of player profiles (goalkeeper and the backline) made the core of the team on which their signature playing style was built. Of course, it's the midfield – and Messi – that truly symbolises the modern revolution, but every attack still begins with the backline, so that quintet of players remaining the only unchanged aspect of the team under Lucho, at least profile-wise, is quite telling and also understandable. But what about the midfield? Xavi's diminishing role and the introduction of Rakitić to compensate shifted the focus elsewhere.

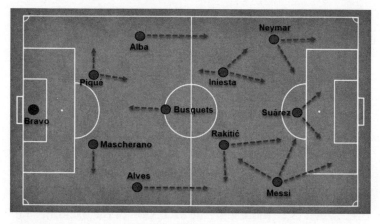

While the trident of Busquets, Iniesta and Rakitić was still a very formidable one, for the first time in years the midfield wasn't where Barcelona's biggest and best players were playing – excluding Messi from the equation, of course. They were still very good but their roles had changed to support a more star-studded frontline. Busquets would still drop deep to aid the build-up and he was still in charge of dictating Barcelona's tempo in the first phase of play. We wouldn't necessarily always see him between the centre-backs, but he was still deeper than the other two midfielders. Iniesta saw his role change as well. Interestingly, he too would start positioning himself slightly deeper, helping carry the ball up the pitch but also still having the freedom to make forward runs beyond the opposition's backline. Both him and Rakitić, however, would also have a supporting role alongside their usual set of tasks.

During his Sevilla days, the Croat was a very aggressive midfielder, even playing as the No.10 just behind the striker. As such, in addition to his good passing, he had a skill set that made him useful within the final third and towards the opposition penalty area too. However, as the front trio's prominence rose, the midfield had to compensate with their movement, focusing more on doing extra work to give the star forwards the freedom they needed to express themselves. This was extremely evident in both Iniesta and Rakitić's roles.

'Luis Enrique's success was achieving the balance between three brilliant forwards and the rest of the team. He deployed Rakitić in some sort of a Messi's bodyguard role and it actually worked!' explained Jordi Costa when describing Lucho's Barcelona. 'Messi's bodyguard' might sound like the latest installation of a rom-com movie but, in reality, it really did help Leo remain as effective and deadly while also not taking too much away from Barcelona's collective stability.

Iniesta was similar, although his case wasn't as extreme as the Croat's. He would still have to drift wide and stay deeper for cover but also had the licence to push forward, utilising his passing range and incredible dribbling to create and exploit space. Rakitić was allowed to do more of what he was used to but as time went on his role was more and more limiting due to the constraints of the MSN trident.

Sid Lowe argues:

> In a way, you have to compensate for things Messi doesn't do by having others do it. You see this with Ivan Rakitić who does so much of the donkey work so Lucho can play with that incredible front three. His role to fill those gaps, to keep MSN at its very peak, to make the rest of it work without them being too exposed was key.

Then we come to the real stars of the show: Lionel Messi, Neymar Jr. and Luis Suárez. At the beginning of their relationship, all three were somewhat different players from the ones they would become by the end of it. Neymar, in particular, would evolve into a completely different profile, while Messi would go from a total player to being the very core of the team. However, somewhere in between, they were three very complementary players, enjoying each other's company both on and off the pitch. The Brazilian was more akin to a traditional winger – fast, direct, deadly in one vs one encounters, and with a touch of samba to his moves. He could hold width easily and create space that way, but since he's right-footed, cutting in and letting Alba overlap was also not a problem.

Following years of the false 9 system, Barcelona finally had a natural striker in the form of Suárez too. He was great on the ball but it was his ability to pin back defences and drag markers out of position that the team, and Messi, valued the most – in addition to his goalscoring prowess, of course. But talking about Messi in this era without mentioning El Pistolero would be doing a huge disservice to the Uruguayan, as Sid Lowe explains:

> We often forget how much of a role Luis Suárez played as the wall Messi played off. All he does is give the ball back but it's also much more complicated than it looks. To hold off the defender, to drop off just right so that Messi can finish. It was often about the ball Suárez would play that would look so simple but it was the ball only Suárez could play. And of course, the personal relationship aspect really matters too.

It's incredibly important to highlight this because Suárez in so many ways enabled Messi to do what he does best. Think of the way the likes of Pedro and David Villa were so good at creating space for the Argentine. Without them, he was drowning in the false 9 role but with Suárez in the team suddenly there was another player who not only was a player of immense individual quality but also a player who understood Messi and his needs on the pitch.

Even with Leo himself, we saw a change once more; not really out of choice, but perhaps more out of pure necessity. Andy West explained:

> There was a great debate on where Messi should play in the Luis Enrique days, especially in the early months with Suárez suspended. It was another one of those milestone games [against Atlético Madrid] where Messi went back to the right wing, Suárez down the middle as the traditional No.9 and Neymar on the left wing. From there, there was no looking back for Barcelona. That was the birth of MSN who became the greatest forward line we've ever seen.

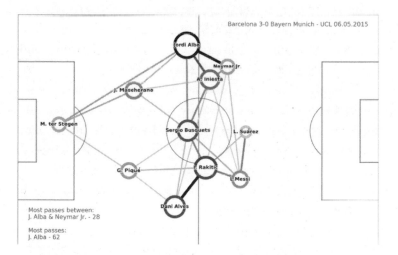

Barcelona 3-0 Bayern Munich - UCL 06.05.2015

Most passes between:
J. Alba & Neymar Jr. - 28

Most passes:
J. Alba - 62

And this pass map from Barcelona's 3-0 victory over Bayern Munich back in 2015 may tell us more about the players' positioning. Due to Messi's preference for the central areas,

Suárez was initially forced out wide. But as I've mentioned before, this didn't work because the Uruguayan is no winger – he doesn't have a lot of pace nor trickery to be an effective Barcelona wide man. Over time, Lucho gradually pushed Messi back to the right-wing position, slotting Suárez back down the middle. And with Neymar completing the trident on the left, the stage was set for a period of domination. It all started with that January clash against Atlético Madrid, as West mentioned earlier, and the Catalans and Lucho would never look back. However, the pass map we can see here is also a great representation of what was actually happening on the pitch.

Neymar and Messi are the wingers but are occupying their respective half-spaces because both had the tendency to cut inside on their stronger foot; the former on his right and the latter on his left. This also inevitably created space for both Alba and Alves to run into. But while the Spaniard is more inclined to attack on the overlap, the Brazilian was more versatile in his approach, swapping between underlaps and overlaps with a plethora of different combinations and patterns alongside Messi and Rakitić on the right.

This also brings us neatly to the midfielders once more. I've talked about their supporting role, and you can actually see it on the pass map too. Notice how both Iniesta and Rakitić are positioned just behind their respective wingers, the former behind Neymar and the latter behind Messi. This is no coincidence. Since the front three were given as much freedom as they wanted or needed, it was the midfield's direct threat that often had to be sacrificed. Iniesta, in particular, is a very good example in this scenario. From the 2014/15 season that saw the birth of MSN, until Neymar's last season, Iniesta's xGChain90 (total xG of every possession the player is involved in per 90 minutes) was at 0.85, and his xA90 (passes

FC Barcelona's Messi (up) and Ronaldinho celebrate their second goal against Albacete during their Spanish League football match at the Camp Nou, 1 May 2005

FC Barcelona's manager Frank Rijkaard with Lionel Messi

FC Barcelona's Ronaldinho (L) Samuel Eto'o (R) hold the trophies of FIFA World Player of the Year and Leo Messi with his Golden Boy trophy before the Spanish League football match against Celta at the Camp Nou stadium in Barcelona, 20 December 2005

Messi runs to celebrate his second goal, UEFA Champions League semi-final game between Real Madrid and FC Barcelona, Bernabeu Stadium

Barcelona's Lionel Messi celebrates after scoring with his coach Josep Guardiola

Barcelona's forward Lionel Messi receiving the European Footballer of the Year award, the 'Ballon d'Or'

Luis Enrique and Lionel Messi during Barcelona's 3-2 victory over Villarreal, February 2015

Lionel Messi and Cristiano Ronaldo during a match between FC Barcelona and Real Madrid

Lionel Messi celebrates with his team-mates Neymar da Silva Jr and Luis Suarez

Lionel Messi celebrates the Champions League victory with his team-mates

Head coach Ernesto Valverde of FC Barcelona congratulates Lionel Messi as he walks off after being substituted

Leo Messi celebrates a goal against Real Madrid

Lionel Messi, his wife Antonella Roccuzzo and their sons

Lionel Messi during his press conference to talk about his departure from FC Barcelona on 8 August 2021

leading to a goal per 90) at 0.20. When we contrast that to his xGChain90 of 0.61 and xA90 of 0.09 in the first season after Neymar's departure, the difference is drastic. Of course, with the Brazilian's exit Barcelona had lost a lot of firepower too, which also affected the midfielder's statistics. But during the MSN reign, the data confirms that the midfield's primary goal was to feed the forwards as opposed to retaining possession and posing danger themselves.

The same was true for Alba, who was largely tasked with only getting the ball to Neymar, as we can see from the pass map from the Bayern Munich match. Alba–Neymar is the biggest connection on the pitch as the two exchanged 28 passes that night. The numbers support the thesis as well. When Neymar was still at Barcelona, Alba's highest xA total (the sum of expected goals from shots from a player's key passes) was 4.67 in 2015/16. In 2016/17 it dropped to 3.68, but the first season without Neymar it skyrocketed to an incredible 6.69 xA. The difference, once again, is quite telling. Alba would, of course, continue rising in prominence, becoming one of Barcelona's main outlets in attack and Messi's best partner on the pitch. In the MSN era, however, that wasn't as evident.

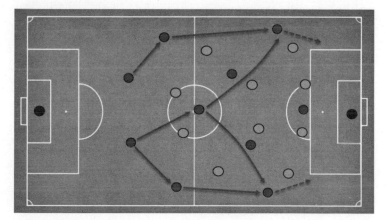

The build-up phase under Luis Enrique was largely based on the premise that the ball needed to get to the front three as soon as possible. In that regard, Pep's patient build-up and 'death by a thousand passes' approach was scrapped for a much more direct and vertical approach. The first phase of attack still started with the backline, as I've mentioned earlier in the chapter, but instead of combining with the midfield and then the trident in the middle of the park recycling the ball until gaps appeared, the ball went straight to the full-backs and then the wingers. The alternative was still finding the pivot or one of the interiors, but their first instinct was to pass to their respective winger. If you go back to the Bayern Munich pass map, you can actually see those sequences unfold.

Notice a very peculiar thing in the graphic – there's no connection between Piqué and Mascherano. The two weren't exactly preoccupied with recycling the ball, but would immediately go for vertical passes or try to find the full-backs. At this point, we have to stop and talk about Messi a bit more.

In this stage of his career, Leo's profile was expanding exponentially and his positioning was starting to become deeper and deeper with each passing season. During the MSN era, he was still very aggressive, pacy and as lethal as ever, but also more involved than before. In his false 9 days, he was the main goalscorer with a hint of a creative side popping up. But now, with Lucho on the sidelines and Neymar and Suárez accompanying him in attack, Leo's creativity would really come to light. He still started very high but would drop to receive the ball from either Alves or Rakitić, two of his very common connections in those years. Often, that would happen around the halfway line or just ahead of it. From that area, Messi would start one of his marauding runs before combining with either Neymar or Suárez up front.

His movement, however, would dictate how his team-mates – and opposition – were structured. Leo's inverted run would prompt Suárez to drift wide and Alves to overlap. On the other hand, if Messi stayed wide and got into a position to cross, Rakitić would charge forward through the half-space. There were a hundred different ways that Barcelona could hurt their opposition, especially with the MSN as rampant as they were at their best.

'A really hard-working, well-structured team. And while the MSN reign was brief, in those six months of their dominance, I've never seen anything like it. The way in which they played, it was just magic,' says Graham Hunter. But it's very difficult to pinpoint very specific sequences in the final third. The build-up is far more predictable and there are little patterns you can discern just by watching them progress the ball up the pitch. For the final third, however, you can certainly do the same but the game plan would differ nearly every time and the scenarios I could list as repeating or unique are far too many to count.

However, it goes without saying that the best Luis Enrique's Barcelona had to offer would include all three of Messi, Suárez and Neymar. So we'll look at a sequence that included all three, while also telling us more about Leo's tendencies in those years. The next graphic is, interestingly enough, from a match against Bayern Munich once more, only it's the 3-2 defeat in Germany a week after the huge 3-0 victory at the Camp Nou.

The thing to note here is the positioning and the movement of players again. The front three are particularly interesting; Messi is in a far deeper position than we were used to seeing, and he's assuming the role of a playmaker who's going to unlock a defensive structure with a single line-breaking pass. Suárez and Neymar, on the other hand, are making excellent runs beyond the opposition's backline, attacking the space inside the

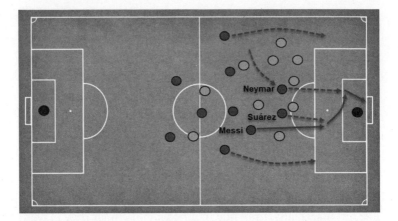

penalty area. Neymar is the one laying the ball off to Messi as he's cutting in from the left, allowing Alba to overlap in the process. We also have Alves in a far deeper position on the other side, but as soon as Barcelona start to quickly advance, he sprints down the right flank into the space Messi has created for him. The sequence ends with a brilliant Neymar tap-in, perfectly executed to bypass the defence almost effortlessly. From Messi's incredible pass and Suárez's run and lay-off, to Neymar's finish past Manuel Neuer, it was like clockwork, and Barcelona would eventually advance past the Bavarians on aggregate despite losing on the night itself.

Ultimately, of course, they would also lift the Champions League trophy come the end of their European campaign. But this is just one of many ways the trio devastated the opposition. Being so extremely vertical and direct in their approach, Lucho's Barcelona had the ability to dismantle blocks in transition, something that the modern iteration of the squad is still struggling to replicate. Messi and Neymar may not have been wingers in the traditional sense, especially the Argentine, but back in those days they had a lot of pace and no trouble covering large spaces rather quickly. When you combine that with the excellent vision and passing range of the likes of Iniesta, Rakitić or even Messi when he was deeper, you get an incredibly potent formula for transitional football. Often, it would indeed start with Leo himself. But, once again, it was all about that directness and the speed with which the ball would always be deployed to one of the front three, whether that was to Neymar hugging the touchline on the left, Suárez dropping slightly for a lay-off before sprinting beyond the opposition's defensive line a moment later, or to Messi waiting to receive and progress with his signature run from the deep. Let's observe one counter-attacking sequence in the following graphic.

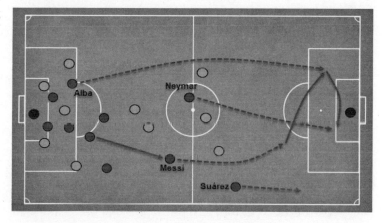

In this scenario, the opposition is on the attack with every Barcelona player defending apart from the front three, which, interestingly, is another big aspect of the MSN era, but we'll come to that a bit later. As the opposition scrambles for the ball inside the Catalan box, a quick pass is played into Messi's feet just around the halfway line. This was a very common area for him to receive in transition, and from there he had the space and freedom to start running at the opposition.

There are actually a couple of aspects we can discern from this single passage of play. Firstly, as already mentioned, upon regaining possession, Barcelona players would immediately look for one of the front three to start the transition. There was no recycling of the ball or trying to escape the immediate counter-press with short combinations, but rather a medium-to-long pass was deployed, in this case to Messi. Secondly, notice the movement of Neymar and Suárez: the former has drifted inside and is now attacking the box through the central channel. As a response to that and to Leo's positioning, the Uruguayan drifts wide, dragging and occupying the marker to free up both of his team-mates. Messi then runs with the ball into the space the other two have created before lobbing the ball into the feet of Alba, which is the third aspect to take note of. The pacy full-back was just coming out of his shell at this point, as we've seen through data earlier as well, and his attacking contributions would only rise over time following Neymar's departure.

The main takeaway is that Alba wasn't the only outlet Barcelona had. All three of the forwards were far more aggressive and willing to attack space than would be the case in the years following MSN's break-up. And this was key, not only for their attacking phase but also for their defending too. Having such an 'unstoppable machine' up front, as Jordi Costa called them, made opposition teams very careful. Even when they were on the front foot and pinning Barça back, they had to leave additional support deeper just to minimise the damage MSN could inflict in transition.

That's the final thing we have to make note of from the previous graphic: there are three defenders staying back to at least match Barcelona's front three, and two just ahead of them for more defence. But, ultimately, even that wasn't enough as MSN tore through them with ease. Speaking of the defensive phase, however, there were some changes in those aspects too, compared to the Pep era that preceded it. Barcelona were still very aggressive, especially in Lucho's first two seasons in charge, and would press high up the pitch to great effect.

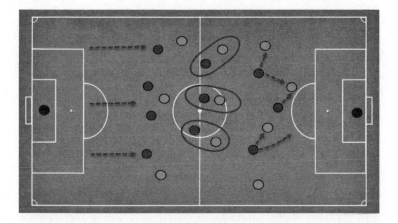

Generally, we saw a very high defensive line again and an emphasis on good counter-pressing as soon as possession was lost. But Lucho's Barcelona were often also very man-oriented in their approach, which was especially true for the midfielders. The forwards, including Messi, would still press high up the pitch, but wouldn't track back nearly as often as was the case under Pep. This is where Leo's defensive work rate, in particular, started to drop significantly. He would hover around the halfway line while the team was in a low block, but was then ready to attack space in transition. So, in that sense, this set-up would still profit from his high positioning, but as he grew older and much slower, the effectiveness of it would wane rapidly.

In the end, the last big thing the MSN trident would do was overthrow that 4-0 deficit against PSG, only for them to fall to Juventus shortly after. It was the beginning of the end for the illustrious trio, as Graham Hunter explained to me:

> Gradually what happened was that Luis Enrique realised the players weren't behaving properly and weren't doing the things he wanted. If you look at him as a national team coach, if anyone fails to do

something he says he drops them, kicks them out, doesn't matter who they are. At club level, you can't really do that so he just got tired out with the whole process.

With the departure of both Neymar and Lucho, Barcelona would start going down a dark path that eventually led to gloom and despair.

Messi, however, had one last trick and one last evolution up his sleeve. This one would take him from a total player and a player within Barcelona's system to being the system itself. But while the individual would still continue thriving to a certain extent, the collective would suffer immensely, ultimately leading to disaster and the end of an era.

Chapter 5

The Alpha & Omega

A Club in Crisis

Even though many may have predicted Barcelona's eventual collapse long before it actually happened, the magnitude of the Catalan catastrophe was still a big surprise. Ever since the departure of Luis Enrique and Neymar, the club has been scrambling to plug holes left and right; every time one problem was seemingly fixed, another would pop up. Sadly, Barcelona have only themselves and their management to blame for that. Calling them a club in crisis at this point feels entirely justified. And in the tug of war between what the fans wanted and what the upper hierarchy thought was best, Lionel Messi was, unfortunately, the one to often suffer the most.

This, of course, wouldn't become apparent until the summer of 2020 when the Argentine decided to depart the club and look for other challenges – a course of action he thought would benefit all parties involved. And for a while, it truly seemed like the end of the road for one of football's greatest love stories. However, Barcelona, or rather Josep Maria Bartomeu, wouldn't allow it. Following a very much drawn-out drama that would put most telenovelas to shame, Leo ended up staying at the club. There's no denying he was forced to do so. After all, the player himself officially requested to be sold and confirmed as much in the interviews following this rollercoaster of global magnitude. But as strange as it may sound, all of it was only the tip of the iceberg in a sea of controversy, corruption and lies that were surrounding the club at the time.

In recent years, there have been so many fires that needed putting out that it's getting increasingly difficult to keep track of them all; when we talk about a crisis, it's completely fair to ask 'which one exactly?' Is it the one Barcelona were facing on the pitch, playing monotone and slow football, bereft of any idea, vigour and heart? Could it also be the financial one, brought upon by the ridiculous spending spree in the market that resulted in the club's debt skyrocketing at an alarming rate? Incredibly, there are far more. For a club with a democratic and perhaps romanticised ownership model led by their members or *socis*, Barcelona were increasingly distancing the club from the fans. It's quite telling that *that* modern period was edging ever closer to becoming the darkest in the Catalans' history, especially considering they had to endure four decades of hardship under a literal dictator in Spain. If that doesn't put things into context, hardly anything will.

But the financial dark hole, the lack of clever spending and the schemes of the upper hierarchy would somehow be swept under the rug and eventually perhaps even be forgotten had the club not forsaken that which they claim is at the core of their very self – *identity*. Such a fragile and yet complex aspect. For Barcelona, it represents their view of the football world and the proper *Azulgrana* way to play the beautiful game – dominant and arrogant but graceful and stylish at the same time.

In the last 20 years or so, we've seen many stars don their colours but, despite that, it was never about any single individual, even if that certain someone was Lionel Messi of all people. Rather, it was always about the power of the collective and how it was superior to anyone willing or foolish to challenge it. The core values passed on by Johan Cruyff, perfected by Pep Guardiola and then tweaked and tinkered with by Luis Enrique were all but gone. And, sadly, it wouldn't take a quick pull of the plaster to heal, either. This downfall has brewed through years of mismanagement, wrong appointments and acquisitions, wrong leaders and even worse principles to break down what was once untouchable. It isn't surprising, then, that Xavi is the fourth coach they've had since 2017, when Valverde first inherited the mantle from Luis Enrique. Of course, we're not counting Sergi Barjuan who was only the interim for ten days, overseeing three matches and thus becoming the only manager in the history of the club never to lose a single match.

This lack of identity, and thus lack of any direction on the pitch, heavily impacted the way in which Messi was moulded as a player. We've seen earlier that he would always adapt to the needs of the team. When Barcelona were at their best, Xavi and Iniesta were running the show in midfield alongside Sergio Busquets. In the modern days, Messi was the one tasked to do it by himself. When they had the likes of Suárez and Neymar in the team, he was willing to share the spoils of war, return to the wings and play his role from there. Now, without them, he had to adapt once more, pulling the strings from deep while also piling the goals on at the other end. It's a very unenviable position to be in, even for arguably the greatest player to have ever played this sport. This inevitably came with a great cost, breeding what's now famously known as the 'Messidependencia'.

Even though this is a term heavily exaggerated in the urban dictionary used by fans, it's indeed a very real phenomenon in Barcelona's legacy. Jordi Costa explains it well:

[After Luis Enrique] Barcelona started to play exclusively FOR Messi, and it's obvious it doesn't work, even if you have the best player of all time. Neither Valverde nor Koeman tried to change this approach and Messi couldn't do all the things he did five years ago. It all became more difficult because he was the only inspiration of the team.

So perhaps unwittingly Messi and his greatness only prolonged Barcelona's road to redemption by papering over the cracks through the sheer power of his abilities and talent. He was still the best in the world, but ironically he was also keeping the team from evolving when it most needed it. Interestingly, Messi himself recognised that to be true. It may not seem so to an outsider looking in but, by wanting to leave Barcelona, Leo wasn't being a captain abandoning his sinking ship, but rather the one trying to save it. 'There was nothing wrong with wanting to leave. I needed it, the club needed it and it was good for everyone,' he said to Rubén Uría in an exclusive interview with *Goal* back in the summer of 2020. Messi knew that, if he left, both parties would suffer immensely but they would also both survive and fight to live another day. Him with PSG, chasing new titles and new challenges, and his beloved Barcelona getting a fresh start with new kids having their chance to shine.

They say that every civilisation is born, peaks and then experiences a downfall. Football works in a rather similar manner – teams start new and exciting projects, soar high up to win it all, and then, following a period of dominance and superiority, they fall, only to be reborn once their time comes again. Needless to say, Barcelona's peak is long gone and it was only through Messi that they've staved off their complete downfall for so long. But it was only prolonging the inevitable as the cracks split open with his departure. Koeman too is now gone, as is Valverde, and Setién; all different coaches who were given an impossible task. All of them were excited to manage the best player in history, only to completely succumb to his power and tremendous influence he has on the pitch.

As we'll see in the following pages, their biggest mistake was not building the team around Messi, masking his deficiencies and enhancing his strengths, but rather wanting to make *him* the team, as Costa alluded to earlier. Álex Delmás puts it beautifully too:

> Nowadays, you can use whatever structure you want, but it's better for Messi to play in the middle and organise the team. However, it has to be a very balanced team. Messi is a player that conditions the collective, mostly in a good sense, but this also has some bad aspects to it. To get the best out of Messi, the team needs wingers, verticality, making the pitch big and someone in front of him to get the attention of the defence and then give Leo space to do his magic.

There's nothing inherently wrong with making Messi the centrepiece; after all, it would be difficult not to rely on the best player on the planet. But putting all one's eggs in the same basket is almost never a good idea, even if that basket turns out to be Messi himself. So, in a way, that was Barcelona's downfall. Quite ironically too, considering the greatest tool in their arsenal might have been the one conditioning their demise. A similar thing might be happening to Manchester United with Cristiano Ronaldo's return – a player who's the answer to so many questions ends up posing far too many himself. Although Messi's case was similar, the context was still different. The bottom line, however, remains the same –

Barcelona and Manchester United were two clubs wielding the power of two of the greatest players of our generation without knowing how to get the best out of them. After all, for all their ingenuity, both players are in their 30s and inevitably come with certain caveats.

Sid Lowe explains:

> It's difficult. In theory, it's always a good plan to give the ball to the best player that's ever lived. In practice, it may not be so. Players can give him the ball too often or in the wrong positions, etc. But a big reason why this was happening is also the emotional importance of Messi – players sort of hid behind him, allowing him to take responsibility, which meant they didn't have to. That might not be a deliberate decision, it's more about if you're going to rely on someone, it'll be that guy.

It's important to have players and coaches who have a clear voice, an agency within the team. With Messi around, it was way too easy to just go on autopilot and hope he would solve whatever issue the team had to face. More often than not, it would indeed be the case. So, in a certain way, that 'dependencia' moulded the whole culture of the club; not just the way they played, but also the way they acted and felt.

The other very important aspect here is how coachable names of such gigantic status are. Were the likes of Valverde, Setién and Koeman even equipped to deal with someone like Messi? Graham Hunter explains the situation:

> He [Messi] is ultra, ultra-demanding and he can only see winning. And, therefore, there were situations where it was difficult to be the coach. I thought Setién

and [Pablo] Sarabia handled it pretty badly, but even though Koeman's tactical ability or the ability to read a game weren't very good, his man-management with Messi revitalised him and made him committed.

So we can say that, yes, Messi has a very difficult persona to manage on the pitch and the training ground; a perfectionist who won't tolerate anything subpar in any sense of the word. It then stands to reason that Barcelona were indeed facing a huge issue, because not only did they need a good tactician to find the structure and build the team around Messi, but that certain someone also needed to have the necessary man-management skills to handle and feed Leo's hunger for success and perfectionist persona.

Was Messi coachable in his final years at the club? I would still argue yes, but if you didn't win him over from the very first moment, it was difficult to come back. He wanted to feel challenged in training sessions, as if the project was always moving forward. Even though their hunger to win may not be exactly the same, Sid Lowe makes the comparison with Michael Jordan in saying that Leo was always driven by the innate desire to be the very best. And if the staff around him, or even the players for that matter, didn't satisfy that hunger and drive of Leo's, problems arose:

> In training sessions, sometimes Messi would turn up in the morning and you could see he's not up for it. And that could torpedo the whole session. Not necessarily because he's trying to torpedo it or directly trying to undermine the authority of the manager or because he's trying to get anyone sacked, but he's looking at his managers and he's just not convinced. And if he's not convinced, he's not convinced. If it

doesn't work for him, he goes 'right, whatever'. So there is a sense Messi can just decide 'well, that's the end of today's session'. He won't necessarily walk off but he simply disengages because it's on his terms. But then he'll come back again and be brilliant, be the best. So it's very, very hard to create an environment in which you impose the same demands on a player upon which the rest of you rely. That in itself becomes problematic over time.

Needless to say, it did become problematic over time. Of course, Messi's importance was such that he became a structural and psychological issue just by being the best. It's quite ironic in so many ways but he truly was both Barcelona's biggest ace up their sleeve and a thorn stuck in their side. That's not to say it was directly his fault. On the contrary, no one would ever ask him to be less good than he was, but having a team to complement his persona and skill set was equally as important as it was never to allow the team to hide behind him.

Sid Lowe explains that Messi himself was often put in those difficult situations precisely because of all the responsibility he would get:

Messi became so big that you create this scenario in which everyone builds towards him. Everyone is frightened of him in a way but not afraid as such. He's not a problem in terms of he's going to shout or scream or tell other players they're useless. It's more about trying hard to keep Messi emotionally engaged and happy, because he's more than capable of just going 'Whatever, forget this …'

For that reason, with everything on him, Messi wielded incredible power in the dressing room and on the pitch. And that also put the coaches at that time in a very unenviable position of catering to his persona while also trying to spread the burden of his responsibilities across the squad.

Lowe continues:

> Messi can be a difficult character but in part because of the high demands he's making. Emotionally it's the strangeness of the situation in which you are so clearly better than everyone else and everyone else so clearly relies on you but, to get the best out of you, you need to cede responsibility to them. But then, it's almost too easy to do it yourself.

It was a task far too big for many who even dared to try. However, try they did, and in the post--MSN and post-Luis Enrique era, Barcelona had gone through coaches like a hot knife through butter, churning out a new one almost every season until they were literally thrown out to prevent riots by the fans. Just as Koeman's car was attacked when he was leaving the Camp Nou, so too were Valverde and Setién downright hated by the end of their tenures in Catalonia.

But what exactly were the structures they tried to implement? All of them were brought in for a reason, and all had a similar idea in mind upon sitting in the hot seat at the Camp Nou – go back to the roots, make La Masia great again and restore the club's lost identity. However, none of them were really successful in the end. With that in mind, we'll touch upon Barcelona's tactics as a collective in the period from 2017 and up to 2021 to see what roles Messi had in them, as well as looking at the next and (so far) final stage of his evolution.

The Metronome

Messi's player profile has evolved tremendously over the years, and while his last epoch at Barcelona isn't significantly different to what we've seen in the MSN era, it's still of great significance. Calling a player the 'alpha and omega' of any team would find most fans, especially of rival clubs, shaking their heads in disbelief. But Messi's last few dances with the *Azulgranas* have largely felt exactly that way. That's what he was in terms of pure ability, superiority and talent, but he was also the 'alpha and omega' of Barcelona in those years because, to put it simply, he *was* Barcelona. We've seen how the tactics of the team sometimes largely revolved around the magic a single player can produce, and that inevitably had an impact on the development of his player profile too.

After the departure of Neymar Júnior and Luis Enrique, the team entered a period of identity crisis, slowly sinking deeper as a collective while Messi individually still managed to shine. But this also prompted more and more involvement across the pitch. He went from a pure winger to a false 9, then to a winger again, and finally to something increasingly akin to a midfield playmaker than a forward. Marsden explained it nicely too:

> In the most recent years we've seen the Messi that's still scoring goals but not as many; he doesn't have the legs, the pace and the trickery which he once had. He's still one of the best in the world, obviously, but this Messi is more characterised by coming deep and his diagonals to Jordi Alba. He's orchestrating more without losing too much in the final third.

We can actually see this in the area Leo occupied when in possession of the ball.

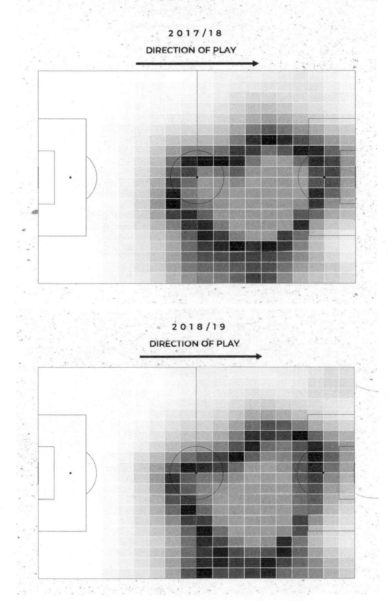

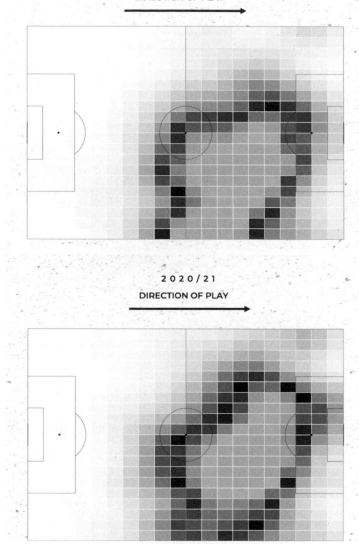

The heatmap can tell us more. Messi's attacking touches are once again edging ever closer to the central channels and he's receiving the ball deeper and deeper on the pitch. As the years went by, the Argentine's heatmap started to spread until it finally covered almost the entirety of the opposition's half – quite literally. The problem Barcelona often faced was how to unlock a deep defensive block. In those instances, Messi was almost always the solution. However, while this deep movement certainly is a big difference compared to his initial player profile, we've actually seen Leo do it in previous chapters too.

But with both Neymar and Suárez on the pitch under Lucho, the Argentine was slowly returning back to his winger role. Of course, we've also seen that even while playing as a winger on paper, he would never again perform that role in the traditional sense of the word, rather inverting and occupying central and deeper areas of the pitch. But with MSN broken up, the major brunt of attacking responsibility was once again his, and his alone.

Starting with the 2017/18 season, we see him spend more time around the halfway line, and, remarkably, drifting across to the left side, which he hadn't done before – here lies his final evolution in movement.

In his prime and false 9 years, he moved across the final third to pull markers, confuse defences and wreak havoc. But in the final stages of his Barcelona career, he moved across to orchestrate attacks from a plethora of deep and diverse positions, now including both flanks. He would act almost as an anchor and deep playmaker who connected the dots and utilised his incredible vision and technique to thread passes most people couldn't even see.

This inevitably affected his chance-creation map, which we'll discuss next.

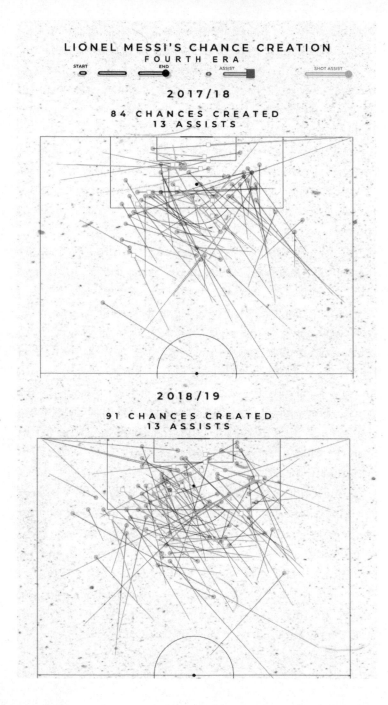

LIONEL MESSI'S CHANCE CREATION
FOURTH ERA

START　　　　END　　　ASSIST　　　　　SHOT ASSIST

2017/18

84 CHANCES CREATED
13 ASSISTS

2018/19

91 CHANCES CREATED
13 ASSISTS

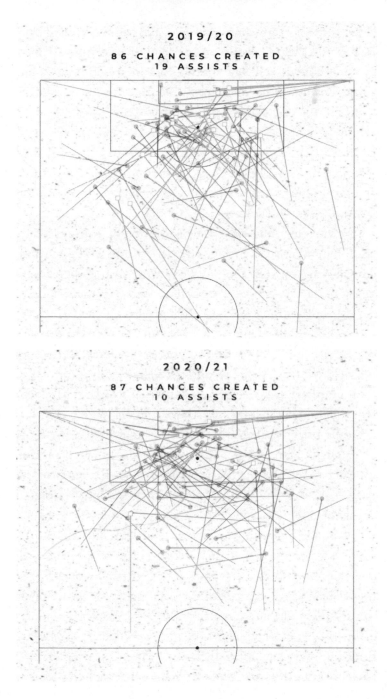

2019/20
86 CHANCES CREATED
19 ASSISTS

2020/21
87 CHANCES CREATED
10 ASSISTS

What started off as a couple of passes and chances created back in 2005/06 became a very common sight by the time 2020/21 was done and dusted. The sheer output increased from season to season too, as he went from 306 chances created in his third era to 348 in the fourth. Similarly, Messi's 52 assists across the four seasons in the third era are bettered by the 55 he added to his tally from 2017/18 until 2020/21. Needless to say, his playmaking skills somehow improved even with the team losing big players and him being tasked to often both create and finish chances.

At the same time, the starting location of both his assists and chances created dropped further down the pitch too, emphasising this need to receive outside of the opposition's block, to then destabilise it through incisive passing from deep. A very similar thing can be said about his carries, which we can see in the following clusters, beginning with the 2017/18 season once more. His return to a far more central and deeper role affected the starting location of his mazy runs too.

Compared to his slightly younger self from the MSN era – or the third era in our case – the carries are interestingly less centrally oriented and also originate somewhat deeper more often than before. This is the direct result of Messi picking up the ball around the halfway line and then attempting to progressively carry it upfield before either deciding to shoot or engaging in short and quick combinations with his team-mates. It's also quite interesting to note the endpoint of those carries.

While the surge of 2013/14 remains prevalent, the fourth era is not only specific for deeper-starting carries but also for the higher-ending ones, which is intriguing, to say the least. We can see that more and more of those carries have an endpoint inside the opposition box despite his overall deep positioning. But while we've established that the fourth-era Messi is drifting back inwards, the starting points of his carries are now located

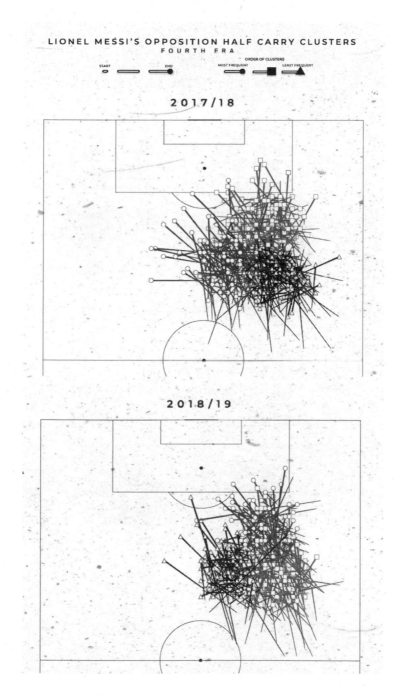

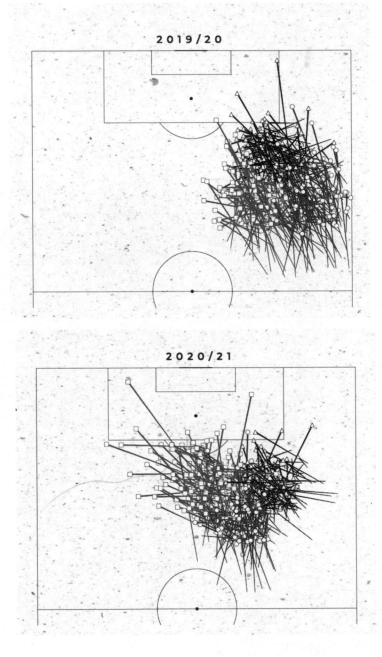

within a far narrower channel, almost exclusively originating in the right half-space. This can be connected to the verticality of the carries too.

Instead of carrying the ball horizontally and more towards either the centre or the flanks like in previous seasons, Messi was now far more vertical in his movement, attacking the box directly.

Probably the best indicator and the biggest difference compared to the third era is in the sheer output. While this increase in quantity started from 2014/15 onwards, it was even more pronounced in the final era of his development. In that sense, Messi was doing very similar things with his carries, only far more often. The same is true for his box entries from the deeper areas.

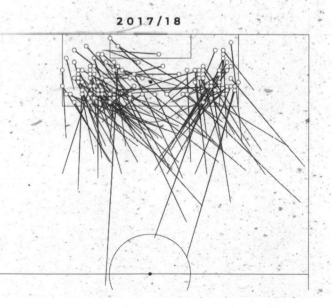

LIONEL MESSI'S OPEN PLAY PENALTY BOX ENTRIES
FOURTH ERA
START   END

2017/18

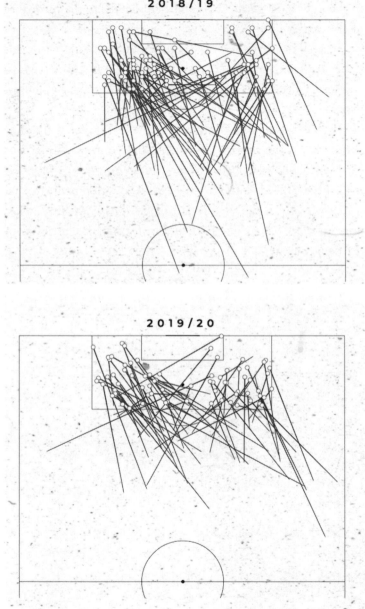

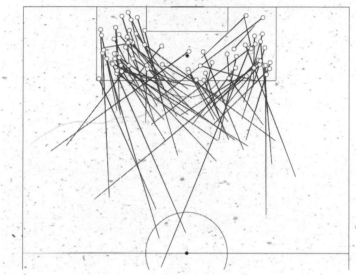

Even though we had started seeing them in earlier years, the numbers increased as the seasons went by, hence a slightly higher figure of entries with very deep starting positions, as can be seen in the graphics. But what about the final product? With his orchestrating responsibilities reaching an all-time high, how did that affect his goalscoring prowess? In short, it didn't – at least, not too much.

Yes, with 126 goals, Messi couldn't eclipse the 134 from the last era. But with the team's collective decline and a much farther-reaching role for him, the eight-goal difference doesn't mean *that* much.

However, Barcelona's increased over-reliance on Messi can be seen in his shooting output. Compared to his 683 shots from the third era, the 725 of the fourth is still a significant increase, especially when considering the non-penalty expected goals values that accompany them. From 2017/18 onwards, Leo had accumulated 78.92 npxG, a significant decrease from the

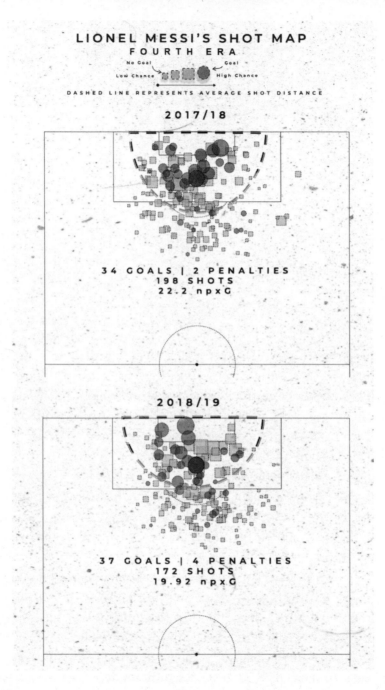

LIONEL MESSI'S SHOT MAP
FOURTH ERA

No Goal — Goal
Low Chance — High Chance

DASHED LINE REPRESENTS AVERAGE SHOT DISTANCE

2017/18

34 GOALS | 2 PENALTIES
198 SHOTS
22.2 npxG

2018/19

37 GOALS | 4 PENALTIES
172 SHOTS
19.92 npxG

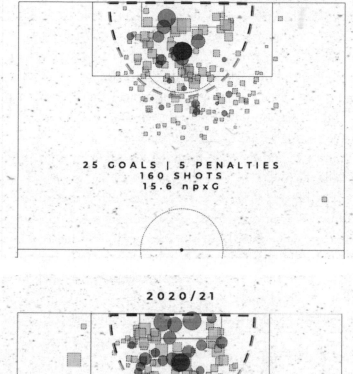

2019/20

25 GOALS | 5 PENALTIES
160 SHOTS
15.6 npxG

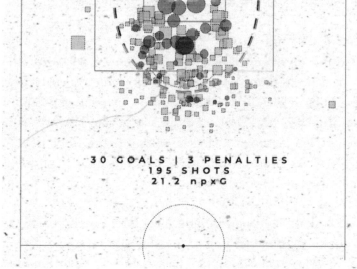

2020/21

30 GOALS | 3 PENALTIES
195 SHOTS
21.2 npxG

89.62 npxG he mustered between 2013/14 and 2016/17. So what does this tell us?

First of all, there's no escaping the fact that Messi was shooting more often and from lower-quality shooting positions, while scoring fewer goals than in the years gone by. Again, this decrease in the final product is heavily linked to the state of the collective. As Barcelona struggled as a team, so did Messi's output. Notice in the shot maps how there are fewer high-quality chances deep inside the opposition penalty area and there are far more lower-quality shots from outside the box.

The biggest difference, by far, lies in the shot distance and overall chance quality. As Barcelona started to struggle more and more with breaching the opposition block, Messi was forced to take lower-quality shots more often, increasing the need for low xG screamers in the absence of much more reliable 'easy' chances.

But what did that look like on the pitch? Let's find out.

The drawing board

Now that we've seen the main characteristics of Messi's profile as explained through the data, let's take a look at some tactical set-ups Barcelona deployed to use his vast arsenal of weapons. Unfortunately, this final era of his stay at the club saw many tactical and personnel changes, so it's difficult to pinpoint a steady pattern. Instead, different coaches tried different things and, while most wanted the same thing, they ultimately went about it in their own ways.

So Messi was deployed in different roles, often either as the centre-forward in a position akin to his early false 9 days, or as the right inverted winger with the freedom to cut in and drop deep. These roles obviously depended heavily on the players Leo shared the pitch with. With Suárez still in the team, Messi would mostly start on the right, but the Uruguayan was at times pushed to the left wing too, making it possible for the Argentine to slot into the central channels.

Soon, the likes of Antoine Griezmann and Ansu Fati came into the picture, as did Philippe Coutinho and Ousmane Dembélé, albeit only occasionally due to his injury woes. But none of that mattered too much. Messi was still the hub of the team in every aspect imaginable – creating, finishing and dictating matches on his own. We'll explore four different traits that were still a large part of his arsenal and look at them through the lens of different matches throughout the years. While the tools we'll analyse are not inherently different from the ones we've seen in past chapters, they're still unique in execution, connections, as well as the movement and areas they originate and finish in.

Let's start with passing. In the previous section of this chapter, we've already touched upon Leo's passing tendencies and the pure numbers behind them, but here we can actually see it in action. Starting from a much deeper area, Messi was a strong transitional tool that could break lines almost effortlessly. Here's a graphical representation of the match against Granada, back in September 2019.

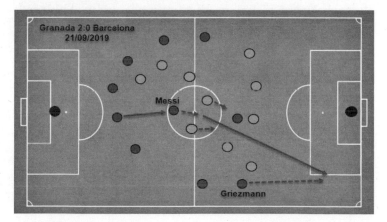

Interestingly, it's a match Barcelona lost 2-0, perhaps somewhat unexpectedly, but Messi still managed to do Messi things that we have to take note of. In this scenario right here, Barcelona are transitioning into the opposition's half with pace and verticality – something that, ironically, they've lacked for years now – but Messi is once again the key cog in the whole sequence.

Upon receiving possession directly from the backline, he takes a couple of steps forward, making Granada's midfield track back and try to plug the horizontal space that he's already easily identified. However, they simply can't react in time, and following a short jog forward with his head constantly scanning the surroundings, Leo spots Griezmann's run along the right flank. The execution that follows is as quick as it's precise and deadly. The Argentine finds his team-mate with a piercing through-ball that breaks lines to create something out of nothing.

And this is a fairly big point too – creating something out of nothing was always Messi's speciality, but never was it more apparent than in the final era we're now analysing. Sure, he was always capable of producing moments of magic, but in the eras of Valverde, Setién and Koeman, that magic was what they often relied upon to win matches or simply survive. This need, and at times downright helplessness of the team, was also what pushed Messi to evolve once again.

Costa explains it well:

> To me, the best quality of Messi is his reading of the game. More than adapting to different structures, I guess he adapted to the qualities of his team-mates. When he had Xavi and Iniesta driving the team, he played nearer the scoring area. Once they left, he started to think as a quarterback, sometimes feeding

[Luis] Suárez up front, sometimes feeding [Jordi] Alba on the left wing. After [Pep] Guardiola's era, he had to get a more global role because the team turned collectively poorer.

And it's exactly the 'global role' that Costa mentions that we're describing here in Messi's final years at Barcelona; the ability to not only put the finishing touches to certain sequences, but also to be at the very beginning of them too. There's a very specific pattern here that we have to analyse and I'll use two examples to make it clearer. The first one comes to us courtesy of a Champions League clash against Slavia Praha in October 2019. Barcelona narrowly edged past their Czech rivals, but were dangerously close to dropping the three points that seemed almost certain before the start of the clash.

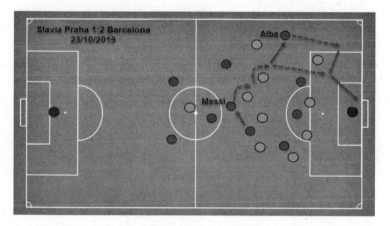

This sequence will show us two very important aspects of Messi's modern profile: dribbling and finishing. Note, however, that this particular action doesn't end up in a goal, but can still offer us valuable insight into how exactly the Argentine operated in such scenarios. Once again, we see Messi start the attack himself, and from a very deep position at that. By this point, the picture is already becoming clearer as most of these sequences do indeed start with La Pulga almost acting as the defensive midfielder and not a prolific forward.

He receives possession from De Jong just around the centre circle, looks up and then the film starts to unroll in his head. The thing with Messi is that he sees these actions unfold at a much higher speed than most of the defenders he faces. He knows where the ball needs to go and how to get it there. Needless to say, the execution is incredible as well. 'He has the technical quality to thread the ball through the eye of the needle but also the vision to see the pass before that. So seeing everything before everyone else,' as Andy West explains it perfectly. Messi takes the ball, beats the marker in his immediate vicinity, then beats another one who comes tracking back in an attempt to stop him, before sending a ball to Alba who's overlapping on the left wing. The pacy full-back runs with the ball for a short distance before sending a telegraphed cut-back to Leo, who hits the target after leaving another defender on the floor.

The most incredible thing about this sequence, however, isn't in the swift one-two between Leo and Alba, nor even in the exquisite dribbling technique on display from the Argentine.

Rather, it's the 'telegraphed' part of it that's crucial. Over the years following Neymar's departure, Messi had created a connection with Alba that even rivalled the one he had with Dani Alves all those years ago, albeit in a slightly different manner. The sequence was almost always the same and it followed two eerily similar courses of action. Either Messi finds Alba directly from a deep position with a pinpoint pass and then the Spaniard attacks the box, or the two combine over a shorter distance, as in the previous example, and Alba promptly returns the favour with a cut-back straight into the

Argentine's feet. Undoubtedly the most impressive aspect of these kinds of actions is their regular occurrence.

This is by no means a one-off, nor is it a moment of magic the two would never replicate. Over the years, they tweaked and perfected it until it was a regular part of Barcelona's arsenal; a weapon everybody is aware of, but can rarely actually stop. That's the beauty of this unique partnership. But another trait of Leo's we have to touch upon here are those late runs into the box. I alluded to this point earlier when I said he started and often finished Barcelona's attacks. The next example, as well as the previous one, do a great job of visualising this.

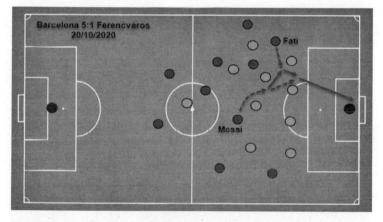

This time we're visiting Barcelona's heavy 5-1 victory over Ferencváros in the Champions League in October 2020. You'll immediately notice how similar this example is to the previous one. Again, we have Messi starting in a very deep position with the Catalans orchestrating another attack against their opposition. Once he receives the ball, the pieces immediately start moving. Leo beats the marker in front of him and continues the run until he can combine with Fati, who's cutting in from the left side. The youngster has but a simple role – set up Leo in a favourable shooting position as quickly and as efficiently as possible. At Barcelona, that usually means within one or two touches at most.

Once the one-two is executed, Messi finds himself around the edge of the box and can attempt a strike on goal. The shot hits the target but fails to hit the net. However, we can still see the late run into the final third from a much deeper position, as well as getting a glimpse at his dribbling, shooting and connections on the pitch. Generally speaking, Fati's role could have been played by someone else, but Alba is the one truly irreplaceable factor in the whole story.

You've noticed many experts mentioning the diagonals from Messi to Jordi and we can't talk about Leo's tendencies without visualising one such sequence to finish off this section. The final and the newest example I'll use for that is Barcelona's 2-1 defeat at the hands of Celta Vigo in May 2021. It's quite telling that many of these latest examples have actually been losses, which helps paint the picture of the real state of the club in recent years. Of course, these are all isolated cases, but they still show a small part of the emerging cracks over time.

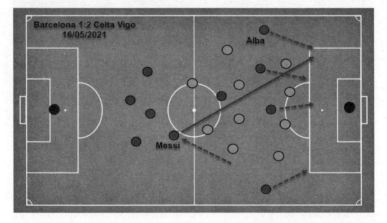

Here we see some very familiar aspects paired up with Messi's incredible passing range. And it's that passing that's seen the biggest evolution over the years. Yes, Leo has improved almost every single facet of his profile since his breakout under Frank Rijkaard, but while many could predict the emergence of the elite finisher, only a few could confidently say he would turn into a world-class playmaker too.

In the example against Celta Vigo, Messi receives possession just ahead of Barcelona's backline, as was often the case.

After a quick scan of his surroundings, he sees Alba making his signature overlap and immediately pings a long, lofted ball into the space ahead of the marauding left-back. The pass is precise, perfectly weighted and advances play in a virtual instant; in other words, it's another classic Leo ball. The fact that one of the world's most lethal forwards has also developed into the world's most creative outlet is as fascinating as it's unbelievable. Messi *is* unbelievable, and yet he's very real.

It's also quite telling that even with such a player, the world's and perhaps history's best, Barcelona stumbled more than they impressed. But with his player profile out of the way, it's time we touched upon the many versions of the collective we saw in that final era, with Leo as the key piece of the jigsaw, of course. Next, I'll analyse Barça's shattered identities in the Argentine's final years (for now) at the club.

Shattered Identities

Lionel Messi's final years at Barcelona were sadly full of disappointment and heartbreak. Although they still managed to find some success early in Ernesto Valverde's tenure, by the end it all still came crumbling down. His successors, Quique Setién and Ronald Koeman, weren't given nearly as much time at the helm simply because their versions of Barça were a step in the wrong direction for so many reasons. But even though we are to criticise all of them, it's also very important to understand this wasn't entirely their fault either. In the years following

Luis Enrique's departure, the term 'Messidependencia' started gaining a lot of traction. The team was increasingly less a stable collective and more a one-man army led by the best player on the planet. The coaches didn't help themselves by not doing much to change this dire fate but it was the upper hierarchy who never made sure the squad complemented the club's needs.

Securing the right type of players is far more important than securing the best players. Even the very best of the best would struggle in systems that don't profit or don't need their profiles, as Graham Hunter explains:

> The [Lionel Messi] dependence increased with the likes of Neymar, Xavi and Iniesta leaving. Yeah, why wouldn't you depend on the best player in the world? But other great players left and the club couldn't reinvent them. You can't just look at the coaches because they don't pick players that are signed. If you look at the players the coaches were given, it's now famous that it didn't really work very well. The club stopped signing players that would've prevented the Messi dependency.

And he's absolutely right too. Of course, coaches can always request certain players, as was the case with Koeman with the 'invasion' of Dutch players. But overall, the board and the president have the final say on the matter, and with many of the superstar signings, you simply knew it was them calling the shots and not the Valverdes or Setiéns at the club.

In that lies the first big mistake Barcelona had made in their modern squad building. Many believe the likes of Valverde and Setién were appointed precisely because of their 'yes-man' personalities as they represented the types of people who wouldn't stand their ground when faced with such controlling bosses. But we're not here to discuss that; we're here to review their tactics, on-the-pitch strategy and, of course, Messi within them.

Still, another big change from years gone by was the amount of money being spent at the club. But even that isn't as simple as it may sound. Yes, Barcelona had spent far too much on players they didn't need, but the market had already changed drastically by that point. It all started with Neymar securing his lucrative and record-breaking transfer to PSG, which completely altered the value of players, forcing clubs to spend far more than ever before. In that sense, spending more was always going to happen, but Barcelona's undoing was spending a lot on the wrong players. Neymar's exit was an unexpected blow that gave the Catalans a lot of money that was burning a hole in their pockets. Other clubs knew that too so they took advantage of Barcelona's obvious panicked state. They had just lost a player they thought would be Messi's heir and they had to replace him quickly. And so the spending spree began.

In 2017/18, with Neymar gone, Barcelona pushed for the transfers of Philippe Coutinho and Ousmane Dembélé, eventually securing both for north of £240m, spending all the Neymar money in what was essentially one fell swoop stretching over two transfer windows within the same season. There were other reinforcements too such as Nélson Semedo or the highly controversial but surprisingly effective Paulinho. Soon, Clément Lenglet joined, alongside Arthur Melo and Malcolm, and then the likes of Arturo Vidal, Antoine Griezmann, Frenkie de Jong and Pedri followed suit. Unfortunately, most of those signings, even the biggest and priciest ones, were complete flops. Three of the biggest ones, however, were Griezmann, Coutinho and Dembélé, together worth over £300m. In a way you can understand the club's desire to try to surround Messi with the best of the best in what would end up being his last years at the club. After all, it was something he himself would have definitely wanted.

Sid Lowe told me in an attempt to somehow make sense of the intricacies of Messi's thinking:

> I think in a way, Messi in his career has probably felt better when the players around him were better and taking some responsibility from him but never taking it completely from him because he wants to feel important. But at some subconscious level he wanted others to take responsibility, obviously wanted a better team around him, everyone does. He wanted to have training that challenged him but didn't always get it. He wanted other players to be better, he didn't want to do it all himself, he didn't want to push out really good players, he wanted them with him.

The thinking behind those superstar signings such as Griezmann and Coutinho was that they would finally be the types of players who could share Leo's burden, taking some of the responsibility on themselves just like Neymar or Suárez before. Ultimately, however, the sheer mismatch in their player profiles didn't allow for that to happen. There were more, of course, some bigger and some smaller signings, but the bottom line is Barça continued buying until there was no more money in the bank and the debt had skyrocketed beyond any sustainable levels. Come 2020/21, one of the biggest brands in world football was completely and utterly broke.

But it was not only the players who came and went. The same occurred with coaches, systems, tactics and other personnel. Barcelona were a mess off the pitch so it inevitably all spilt on to it as well. For that reason, it's very difficult

to pinpoint just one steady line-up across the years as a lot was changing very quickly. Apart from Neymar and Javier Mascherano, the other names being axed were mostly still fresh signings that didn't work out one way or the other. This trend would continue season upon season and many of the arrivals wouldn't last more than a campaign or two at the Camp Nou. Those who did were either loaned out somewhere along the way or simply remained to lurk around because of the club's inability to shift them effectively. Still, even though all the coaches between Luis Enrique and Xavi tried to implement changes, the 4-3-3 formation remained Barcelona's staple, for better or worse. However, arguably the bravest and most successful of them all was Ernesto Valverde.

The former Athletic Club gaffer was always seen as a heavily pragmatic coach, and he may very well have been one, but early in his tenure he wasn't afraid to stir things up. Frank Rijkaard's brainchild was the utilisation of Ronaldinho and young Messi, Pep's was the false 9 in a revolutionary positional heavy system, Luis Enrique's was the balanced team with the MSN trident, and Valverde's was, controversially, scrapping the 4-3-3 for a drastically different 4-4-2 diamond. Others had used different systems to great effect too. Even though both Pep and Lucho weren't afraid to deploy the 3-4-3, for example, the 4-4-2 was considered to be entirely another spectre to what Barcelona were preaching – but it worked.

'I thought Valverde did a brilliant, brilliant job. I thought he found balance, made the team successful and understood what was needed not only for Messi but also for Suárez,' said Hunter. Valverde's Barcelona would soon start playing a very different style to the one everyone was accustomed to. Or rather, they still nourished some of the core aspects of positional play, only they went about it in a slightly altered manner.

The onus was still on possession, but compared to the highly vertical and direct approach of Luis Enrique, Valverde's was slower and more methodical but also, at times, not as effective.

The core of the build-up phase, however, remained mostly unchanged. Everything started with the centre-backs and the defensive midfielder – in this case, Lenglet, Piqué and Busquets. The three of them would often be the deepest players on the pitch, looking to deploy short combinations to advance up the field. With the lack of natural wingers of any kind and a very narrow diamond structure at the beginning of Valverde's tenure, the width was exclusively provided by the full-backs, namely Jordi Alba and Sergi Roberto or Semedo. For that reason, we saw both very high up the pitch, Alba even acting as a winger, considering the time he had to spend in the attacking third.

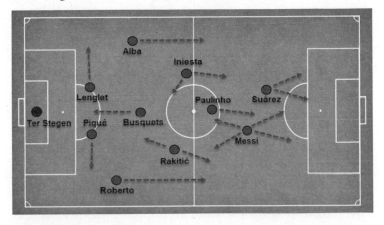

Of course, while creating width and verticality exclusively from the full-backs isn't ideal, Alba's connection with Messi made it worth the effort. This is the era when the two really started to click, even carrying the major brunt of Barcelona's offensive threat. The other two midfielders were still Andrés Iniesta and Ivan Rakitić, but with the former getting on in age and the latter fully transformed into a box-to-box support player, the need for Messi's creativity was bigger than ever. The Croat wouldn't make those darting half-space runs that often anymore and would instead slot behind Leo or alongside him for potential overloads. Similarly, without a proper winger or a natural attacking full-back occupying the right side of the pitch, we would see Rakitić and Roberto often try to compensate for that with their presence on the flank, but neither could really provide the width and the verticality Barcelona needed. The inclusion of Paulinho was also very interesting and I'll touch upon his role in more detail shortly. He was by far the most aggressive of the midfielders and would assume high and wide positions depending on the team's needs.

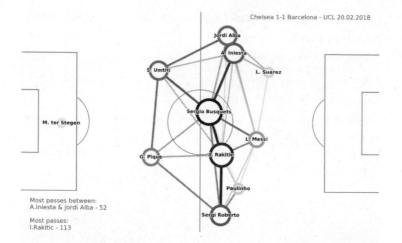

Chelsea 1-1 Barcelona - UCL 20.02.2018

Most passes between:
A.Iniesta & Jordi Alba - 52

Most passes:
I.Rakitic - 113

This pass map against Chelsea in the Champions League is a good example that will tell us more about some possible connections on the pitch. We can see that Busquets is once again at the very core of the team, funnelling play through the middle and having a very strong connection with the centre-backs. Notice Rakitić here as well though; in this example, he actually makes the most passes as his role of an aggressive final third presence is slowly transitioning into one of a ball retainer and possession recycler. Again we come back to that 'Messi's bodyguard' reference from earlier. Instead, it's the new arrival Paulinho who's tasked with breaking the lines with his runs and providing a presence in and around the opposition's box. In the Chelsea pass map, he's positioned to the far right, providing an outlet alongside Roberto and helping to create overloads with Messi.

This brings us naturally to the role of the forwards. Suárez is the nominal striker in the team and he was tasked with pinning the backline, attacking the box and enabling Messi. The Argentine, on the other hand, operated just behind the Uruguayan and was largely given the freedom to do what he wanted to do. Some of his strongest connections involve all three of the midfielders in a slightly deeper role, behind Suárez but almost in line with both Iniesta and Paulinho. The fact that the main recyclers and the more advanced midfield options were constantly looking for Messi tells us enough about the team's need to have him involved as much as possible.

Andy West recalls, telling me about Leo in the final stages of his Barça career:

> In the latter stages of his career, he really started focusing on build-up, joining up playing, linking up with the midfield and playing much, much deeper on the pitch. And that's also connected to the inevitable ageing process, losing the acceleration and the pace. But he's developed his game to compensate for that.

Yes, Messi was getting older too, so losing that pace, stamina and resilience definitely played a part in his evolution, but so did the needs of the team as a whole. With Suárez's output decreasing and the creativity of the midfield slowly declining too, the dependence on Messi's goals and assists rose to unsustainable heights. In Valverde's first season, the Argentine's team goal contribution (goals + assists) jumped from 39 per cent to 46 per cent, reaching the era's highest percentage of 54 in 2018/19.

The problem was starting to become apparent, to say the least. At that time, however, Barcelona's 'one-man army syndrome' didn't stop them from being successful. Valverde managed to get the best out of Messi by setting the stage for him to shine once more. Although Suárez wasn't as deadly, he was still making the necessary movement to free up Leo's preferred spaces. And Paulinho, for all the 'deficiencies' in his profile as a prototype Barcelona midfielder, complemented Messi perfectly. His aggressive runs would not only drag markers away but also gave Leo a target to look for inside the final third and the opposition's box. That's why Valverde put the Brazilian at the tip of the midfield diamond, allowing for a crafty interchange between him and La Pulga.

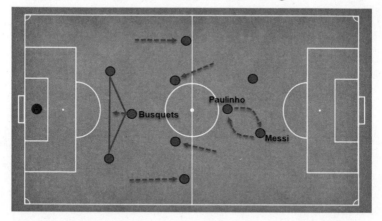

Since Messi's creativity was heavily needed in deeper areas, he and Paulinho would regularly swap places. That way, Messi could combine with the midfield while the Brazilian made forward runs and accompanied Suárez higher up the pitch. With a nose for a goal, both inside and outside the box, Paulinho was the perfect counterweight Barcelona needed while Messi was operating in far deeper areas.

Speaking of the deeper areas, under Valverde and then moving beyond him too, Busquets went back to being the hub of the team in the first phase of build-up play. Under Lucho, that role was somewhat diminished due to Barcelona often skipping the midfield entirely in their search of the devastating MSN trident up front. Now, however, with the emphasis back on recycling the ball, Busquets would come into his own, only this time it would almost exclusively happen while positioned in between the centre-backs. It could be argued that this limited his incredible on-the-ball ability and vision but, despite a lot less technical quality in the middle of the park,

Sergio's stability ensured Barcelona could still stay true to their possession-heavy style.

Iniesta's role was also quite interesting here. He would still drift wide and step forward to create, but now he would cover a far smaller area of the pitch. This was partly due to ageing but also because of Messi's involvement. When positioned deep, Leo assumes the role of a recycler, progressor and creator all in one. He would often drop to receive the ball from one of the midfielders or directly from the backline and then either run forward with it or try to find long diagonal switches to Alba. We've seen such situations in the earlier chapter on his player profile. But since Barcelona lacked any kind of natural width apart from the pacy Spaniard, tactics such as 'overload to isolate' were very prominent. The main idea was to use the likes of Rakitić and Roberto to create overloads on the right and then let Messi use his vision to find an isolated Alba on the left.

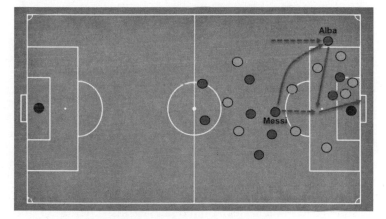

This particular graphic shows us a goal Messi scored against Tottenham Hotspur in the Champions League. Here we see the famous Messi–Alba connection but also some other very important aspects that made plays like this one possible in the first place. Leo starts the attack by deploying a long switch to Alba, who's running into space on the left. Firstly, this shows us

Messi's initially deep positioning and pinpoint passing to find an isolated target running towards the opposition box. Secondly, we see the connection between the two as Alba deploys a cut-back right into Messi's feet for the Argentine to slot the ball past Hugo Lloris for a soft and precise finish. However, there's a third and maybe even most important detail we simply can't overlook here – the runs of both other players in the box. It's actually Suárez and Coutinho whose aggressive movement occupies the defenders and allows Messi the space and time he needed to score; this is at the very core of the post-MSN era.

The team was largely revolving around setting the stage for Messi to take over matches and guide them to victory. We may ponder whether this is indeed an ideal solution but the fact remains, it worked … for a while. In that 2018/19 season, we would see Valverde shift back to the traditional 4-3-3 with Coutinho or Dembélé playing alongside Messi and Suárez in a front three. However, with the Frenchman's constant injury woes, the Brazilian was the chosen one more often than not. But he also wasn't a natural winger and nor was Messi. That meant both would inevitably position themselves more centrally, sometimes stepping on each other's toes and lacking efficiency and any complementary aspects. The dependence on full-backs for width rose once more and Barcelona's central-heavy approach started to cost them results. Soon, Valverde had no way out and new signings didn't help alleviate this problem either.

Another very prominent issue was player selection. The Basque coach had a clear preference for his starting XI and would rarely rotate, even mid-game when it was blatantly necessary. This inevitably led to burnout for one of the oldest variations of Barcelona in a long time, ultimately resulting in disaster, especially in Europe. The fan backlash and unconvincing performances led to Valverde's sacking and prompted Barcelona to shuffle the deck once more. After his departure, Barcelona appointed Setién, who had apparently been on their radar for a long, long time.

The former Real Betis manager was someone who understood the way the squad was supposed to play but his inexperience at the highest of levels and inability to control the biggest stars on the team were his undoing. Sadly, since his stint was far too short to make any significant changes, and although there were some, I won't go into detail on his version of Barcelona. Instead, we'll now turn to the man who took over after him. With Setién gone, in came Koeman, a club legend with a reputation as a harsh man-manager – the complete opposite of his predecessor's personality. On the face of it, it was just what the good doctor had ordered. And for a while, Barcelona were back on track.

The changes Koeman instilled upon taking over were perhaps not seen to be as radical as Valverde's but they would still reshuffle the team quite a bit. Youngsters such as Fati, Pedri, Ronald Araújo and Óscar Mingueza started emerging and taking over the team. With Valverde and Setién out of the picture too, players such as Rakitić, Suárez, Semedo and Melo would follow suit, leaving Barcelona with some new kids on the block. Sergiño Dest, Miralem Pjanić and Francisco Trincão were quickly joined by Memphis Depay, Yusuf Demir and Emerson Royal as Koeman started to piece his jigsaw together. However, none of them would prove good enough to reverse Barcelona's fortunes, a harsh verdict that sadly includes Koeman himself. All three of the Catalans' superstar signings – Coutinho, Griezmann and Dembélé – were still at the club but weren't being put to much good use. Koeman's initial idea was to diverge from Barcelona's traditional 4-3-3, a thought many of his predecessors had too, but he opted for a 4-2-3-1 structure akin to the one we saw with the Netherlands under his watchful eye.

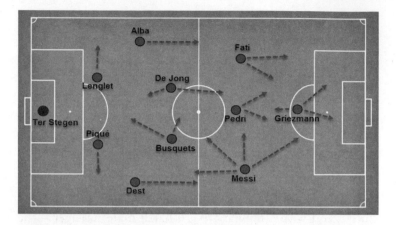

We have to note that the personnel didn't change too much. The backline mostly remained the same, at least for the early stages of Koeman's tenure, with the exception of Dest on the right. The former Ajax youngster arrived as an attacking option that could provide the team with some much-needed width and verticality on that flank. With Messi still being utilised as the right-winger on paper, a good attacking full-back was needed to fill his void once the Argentine inevitably drifted away from that position. The big change here, however, is in the double pivot deployed in the middle of the pitch. De Jong and Busquets were the chosen duo and, in theory, the latter would drop far deeper and stay there for longer, while the former had more of a box-to-box role. The Dutchman was given the flexibility to support the build-up in the first phase and then carry the ball into the final third through his progressive running.

However, even the inclusion of the massively talented former Ajax player didn't completely solve the Messi dependency issue. The Argentine would still drop very deep to collect the ball and look to advance himself, playmaking in the process. We've already seen in his player profile chapter how his positioning was becoming increasingly akin to that of a midfielder.

Contrast that to when he was younger and you see that while he was always cutting in and dropping deep, it was never this far back, and never exactly with the intent of pure build-up and progression. Back then it was more about repositioning on to his stronger foot and attacking the box from a more central position, giving him better shooting locations.

The inclusions of both Fati and Pedri are very important too. The former is someone capable of holding the width and providing vertical runs but also cutting inside and generating a threat inside the opposition's box. That blend of skill and a fitting profile will no doubt be useful for Barcelona in the years to come, but sadly Messi didn't get to share the pitch with the young talent for too long.

Pedri is a similarly promising and fresh addition to a struggling team, and Koeman used his between-the-lines presence to a very good effect. When it comes to Messi's positioning, however, it varied between being deployed on the right wing or centrally, which would then inevitably move Griezmann around too while he was still at the club. But regardless of where he was on paper, Leo would still assume a very deep role in the build-up phase and then look to create from there, either through incisive passing or carrying the ball and combining in and around the box. But

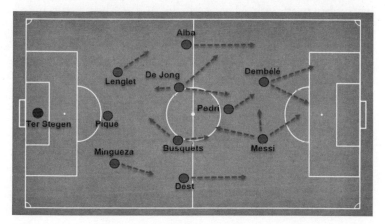

Koeman's 4-2-3-1 and most of its variations didn't stick for too long. Soon, he began an experiment with a three-at-the-back system, using versions of a 3-4-3.

The back three was designed with greater stability and balance in mind. In theory, this would allow Barcelona to achieve numerical superiority without dropping Busquets too deep and, in turn, would allow him to combine with the rest of the players higher up the pitch. Interestingly, Setién had a similar idea despite not deploying a back-three system. His initial thoughts were to keep Busquets closer to Messi as the midfielder had the vision and technique to find Leo in almost any scenario, despite the opposition's best efforts to stop it. De Jong saw a revamp of his role too, sometimes even slotting into the backline as the left centre-back, akin to his Ajax days. Next, Alba and Dest were given far more aggressive roles, now functioning as wing-backs with less defensive responsibility with the coverage of three centre-backs in the backline behind them. But with Pedri occupying the spot just behind the front two, this structure sometimes resembled a 3-4-1-2 instead of a pure 3-4-3.

Interestingly, around that time, Koeman also experimented with Dembélé down the middle, aiming to maximise his pace in combination with Messi's vision. We've already discussed how that's the ideal profile to surround Leo with, and had the Frenchman stayed fit for the majority of his stay at the Camp Nou, Barcelona could have been far more successful despite their ongoing struggles. Without him, the 3-4-3 with wing-backs didn't solve their width issues for good. Yes, Alba and Dest seemed well suited for their offensive roles, but the right side of the pitch remained a problem with Messi so predominantly central and deep all the time.

But a Barcelona team with Leo was never really going to struggle in the attacking phase *that* much. As limited as they were with no width and no real outputs other than the Argentine, they were still scoring goals, albeit not in such incredible fashion as the Barcelona of old. Instead, the issues were far too big to cover off the ball. In this last era of Messi's development and in his last years at Barcelona, the Argentine was completely free of any defensive responsibility. Every new coach to come had tried to implement high-pressing tactics in the defensive phase of the game but would soon find it way too hard to sustain. Partly, this was due to the high average age of the team, but also because pressing is a strategy that you have to commit fully to and act as a compact unit.

Ralf Rangnick said famously via The Coaches' Voice:

> You need to be aware of what kind of football you really want to play. A little bit of pressing? Come on, what is a little bit of pressing? A little bit of pressing is like a little bit of pregnancy. Either you are pregnant or not. Either you want to play with high pressing or not.

Barcelona's issue was that they weren't fully committed to pressing and often left gaps good teams could easily exploit. This inability to replicate Guardiola's efficiency off the ball and the 'six-second' rule led to them utilising a mid 4-4-2 block more and more often. We had seen this under Valverde, but also consistently whenever their high press was broken.

This is an example from when Messi and Suárez were still playing together. Both of them would often remain as the highest players on the pitch, something akin to Ronaldinho and Samuel Eto'o back in Frank Rijkaard's days. But with both of them being much older at this point in their careers, we hadn't seen much effort to disrupt the opposition's first phase of build-up. Suárez would try to curve his runs in such a way

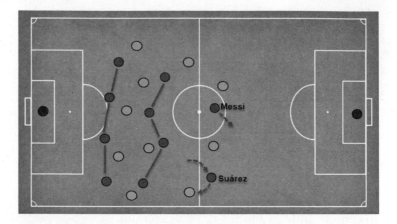

as to split the pitch in half, decreasing the space the other team had to play in, so there was still some thought being put into it.

However, the issue was Messi's largely loose role alongside him. Just the fact he wasn't always applying pressure or wouldn't apply it consistently throughout the match was a problem for the collective as a whole. But then we come back to the initial issue of poor planning and transfer business; Barcelona were not only ill-prepared to move on from Messi, but they were also very ill-prepared to prosper alongside him. Many would say the sheer 'Messidependencia' was at the core of their issues and maybe that's not that far off the mark. However, his departure from the team revealed all the cracks, ultimately ending in Koeman's sacking too.

By the time you read this, the world will have seen the early fate of Xavi's Barcelona as well. Sadly, it will be a Barcelona without Messi, at least for the time being. That, however, doesn't mean his story ends there. His playing career might still take him back home to the Camp Nou but, even if that does happen after his stint at PSG, what kind of a player can we expect to show up at Barcelona's doorstep?

Epilogue

The Curtain Call

ONE OF the jobs of an analyst or scout is to try to predict future outcomes. This applies to both assessing collectives and individuals. Having the knowledge to accurately depict how a team will perform is key to outplaying them. Similarly, having the knowledge to accurately depict how a player will fit a certain system or a league is key to successfully incorporating them into the squad. Assess them wrongly and you end up with potentially future-defining losses. One such scenario ultimately led to Barcelona losing Lionel Messi of all people, an outcome not many could have successfully predicted years before either. Excessive spending on players that didn't fit led to debts, and debts led to the Catalans having to make drastic decisions.

But along those same lines, predicting what comes next for Messi is a very difficult thing. Not many could have confidently said they always knew Leo was going to become an elite creator. Dribbler? One hundred per cent. Goalscorer? Absolutely. But one of the best passers of the ball? Not likely.

Admittedly, at 34, there's usually not much evolution left for most players, even the very best of the best. But one thing his heartbreaking departure from Barcelona showed us is Messi in a different team, a different system and an entirely different environment. It also showed us what won't work for him in the remaining years of his career. At the time of writing this book, Messi is still in the very early stages of his PSG career and by the time this is published, he very well may have either flopped – as much as Messi can flop at anything – or managed to find his footing. But the first couple of months at Parc des Princes were also a cautionary tale for Mauricio Pochettino.

Some things I think are likely by the summer of 2022 are Pochettino getting sacked, Kylian Mbappé joining Real Madrid, and Neymar and Messi staying to see out the rest of their contracts despite not achieving much outside of domestic success, so changes are more than likely. However, one thing Pochettino managed to show us clearly is how *not* to use Leo. His PSG usually deploy variations between 4-2-3-1 and 4-3-3 but it's hardly about the formation here; it's all about the role you assign to Messi. With only parts of 2021/22 to work with, it's difficult to fully assess this stage of his career. Ideally, we would wait for at least a season to see what exactly – if anything at that future point – had gone wrong. However, looking at just over 1,500 minutes of Messi in a PSG shirt can still show us *some* aspects of his potential future development.

Pochettino made a grave mistake at the beginning of Leo's stint in France by deploying the Argentine far out on the right. Of course, by now, we know that Messi isn't a true winger. The same thing could be argued throughout his career, even stretching as far back as his first years as a Barcelona senior. Holding width wasn't necessarily a problem for the younger Messi, though, but it is for a 34-year-old Messi. Hugging the touchline is something he can and will do but only if he's then allowed the freedom to cut inside and position himself more centrally and overall closer to goal. At PSG, at least in the early stages, that hasn't been the case.

This rather drastic change in his approach to games does suggest it's an instruction rather than something he's decided of his own volition. Deploying Messi as a winger when he doesn't make penetrative runs off the ball and can't beat markers over larger stretches of the pitch doesn't make much tactical sense.

Albert Blaya explained:

> Messi will ideally finish his evolution as a second striker, someone with freedom but who must always receive close to the rival area. He needs to have a lot of players in front of him who can help dismark him and create space. The closer to the rival area, the better!

This, needless to say, is a far cry from what we've initially seen at Paris Saint-Germain, where Messi the winger isn't someone with positional freedom, nor is he someone who's as close to the opposition's box as possible.

If you're forcing Leo to cover a lot of ground, you're minimising the threat he can produce. His 2021/22 heatmap across all competitions with the *Parisiens* looks similar to his usual heatmap but with a big exception – he starts by hugging the touchline and spends far too much time there. Note, however, that this is true for the early stages of the campaign and may change by the time you're reading this book. We shouldn't completely disregard the winger position, though. In a more inverted role with the licence to cut inside but do so higher up the pitch, it *can* and *should* work. The final years at Barcelona saw him do the same, even if he was dropping far too deep. Altering the role so that he still inverts but does so closer to the final third would look to maximise his output while still utilising his creative spark. After all, we saw him do that to a similar effect during the MSN era under Luis Enrique when he returned to the right-wing role.

With a star-studded team, especially up front, PSG can still be successful, win Ligue 1 and dominate domestically while not necessarily adhering to the conditions we've just listed. But in Europe, the cracks may begin to show. This wouldn't be solely because of their misuse of Messi, but having him in the squad and not getting the best out of his profile is clearly a problem.

So we've definitely eliminated the natural winger role as the next step in his development. At this point, it's difficult to see him transition to something he left behind all those years ago. His diminishing physique is probably the biggest factor in the whole conversation, with mobility the focal point. Messi operates in bursts and spends huge portions of the game walking. For most players, this would be seen as a liability but football isn't exactly about how much you run but whether you can run smartly. For Leo, the answer to that question is a resounding yes. However, not all players in all roles get that kind of freedom. Running smartly is something everyone should employ, but it doesn't mean everyone can spend a vast majority of their game time walking, or jogging at best.

This is the main reason why I don't believe Messi will ever transition into a natural midfielder. His vision, passing range and overall reading of the game can match the elite playmakers of the footballing world but his work rate is nowhere near the required level. Messi simply doesn't have the legs for a box-to-box role, and deploying him in midfield would likely disrupt the balance of the team. Even when he's an inverted winger or a false 9 devoid of defensive responsibility, it still requires the rest of the team to compensate. The modern game has evolved into a far more aggressive style, both off and on the ball. That means pressing has never been as popular as it is now. But pressing is also a collective aspect. In other words, it doesn't work unless everyone does their part.

Messi can help, sure. But he can't sustain it for long – nor would that be an efficient way to use his energy. Therefore, a midfielder who doesn't work off the ball is more likely to be a liability as much as his creativity would help the team. Messi rarely takes more away from the team than he gives, but in that role there's an argument to be made about it. Luckily, the midfield is a very broad term. If there's a role in the middle of the park that would potentially suit him even in the final years of his career, then it's the No.10 or the attacking midfielder. Messi loves to roam the pitch and this would enable him to drift to either side and drop deep when he deems it necessary. That way, overloads could be achieved through his movement and he would get to create play from deeper areas as well, not to mention that the No.10 role is also naturally more attack-minded, so it would inevitably take him closer to the opposition goal while also potentially minimising his defensive responsibility.

However, even with this role, there are caveats. The only way teams are going to fully reap the benefits of Messi positioned in a slightly deeper central position is if they complement his profile with runners. With players who aggressively attack space ahead of him, Leo can be as deadly as ever without ever scoring goals. I can easily see him thriving and continuing to be a highly influential figure in world football for years to come if profiles compatible with his own can be found within his squad. That, needless to say, isn't always an easy task, but could become a prerequisite for anyone wanting to build a squad with him in it.

Along very similar lines is the second-striker role we've shortly touched upon earlier. This, together with the false 9 and the No.10, is the most likely scenario in my opinion. All three come with a certain dose of freedom, both to move as he pleases and to be an impactful creator and finisher in one. In that sense, we won't exactly talk about another evolution of his profile, but rather an extension of what we've been seeing in the last couple of years. Less ground coverage, fewer marauding runs from the halfway line, but more bursts higher up the pitch, more diagonal and through passes and more smart finishes in and around the box. As far as those aspects of his future career go, that's probably the easier part to try to predict: whether successfully or not remains to be seen, and may even be answered by the time you read this.

The more difficult part is predicting where Messi's journey will take him next. Is it Major League Soccer in the US? Retirement? Back to Argentina? Or perhaps a surprise return to Barcelona if the Catalans can *somehow* balance their books? And that's a big 'if'. At this point, it's anyone's guess. I wouldn't rule out him honouring the PSG contract and then either spending a year or two across the pond before playing in Argentina for fun or retiring soon after that. A return to Barcelona, at least in a player role, is difficult to imagine at this particular point in time.

The truth is that his departure from Barcelona will hopefully spark a much-needed revolution at the Camp Nou; the separation was as necessary as it was painful.

But the way it was done was wrong. The greatest player in the club's history – and potentially in the sport's history – should never have been thrown out the back door. No big farewells, no ceremonies, no heartfelt last applause from the stands. Only tears and regret in one final press conference. Sadly, that's the bitter taste of his departure that will no doubt remain for a long, long time.

But regardless of that, Messi's legacy is something that will outlive us all. He may not be finished yet, and whether there's another evolution around the corner or not, football still owes him a great debt. We can analyse him all we want, dissecting the minutiae that made him the otherworldly footballer he is, but in the end, the best we can do is simply enjoy him while we still can. Football careers are often short and curtain calls are rarely joyful. But Messi? Messi's legacy is forever.

'Don't write about him, don't try to describe him, just watch him,' said Pep Guardiola famously. And that may indeed be the best thing to do in the sunset of Leo's career.

Appendix

Pitch Grid

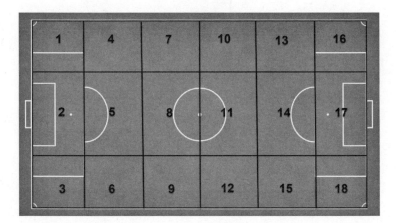